If you are strugg
addiction, please know that it is okay to ask for help.

NATIONAL SUICIDE PREVENTION LIFELINE

suicidepreventionlifeline.org
800-273-8255

ALCOHOLICS ANONYMOUS (AA)

aa.org
212-870-3400

AL-ANON

al-anon.org
888-425-2666

ALATEEN

al-anon.org/newcomers/teen-corner-alateen
888-425-2666

NARCOTICS ANONYMOUS (NA)

na.org
818-773-9999

SEX AND LOVE ADDICTS ANONYMOUS (S.L.A.A)

slaafws.org
210-828-7900

A LIFE OF OPPOSING FORCES

A LIFE OF OPPOSING FORCES

MICHAEL S. MILLIN
with Danielle Makenna Forras

A LIFE OF OPPOSING FORCES

FIRST EDITION

ISBN 978-1-5445-4707-7 *Hardcover*
978-1-5445-4706-0 *Paperback*
978-1-5445-4708-4 *Ebook*
978-1-5445-4705-3 *Audiobook*

To my parents,

may all your pain be turned into a gift for others.

CONTENTS

This is the story of my life. Names, locations, and identifying characteristics have been changed along the way, and in some cases, multiple individuals have been merged into a single character, but the story remains true. The narrative and conversations have been re-created from memory to convey the most honest representation possible. It's a story of generational trauma, the truth about addiction, and relationships. Some of those relationships have stood the test of time, whereas others require repair. It is also a story of recovery, the healing properties of water, and adventure.

FOREWORD

—By Danielle Makenna Forras
Partner, Businesswoman, RYT 200®
Yoga Instructor, Health Coach

There were many things about Michael that surprised me when I met him. It was more than just being impressed watching him surf; I was in awe of his honesty, the way he openly shared his story without downplaying his struggles or hiding behind shame. He owned his battles, his most commonly fought adversary being himself, and he skimmed over his achievements with a level of humility rarely seen. I was taken aback by his level of perseverance and absolute determination to see the world on his own terms, but more than anything, I was blown away by his refusal to compromise his morals for a shortcut or to make life easier.

It's hard to express how important strength of character is to me or how rare it is to find that in people. It's easy to say that we wouldn't compromise ourselves to get ahead. We all like to think that, but when push comes to shove, I have seen so many people weasel their way through life, selling bits and pieces of themselves just for a chance to get ahead, to be known. As you read Michael's story, as you learn about the hardships he has faced throughout his life, you will see how impressive this actually is. You will come to understand how easy it might have been to give up, to give in, rather than to keep going. These types of people, with unwavering strength of character and senses of justice, are few and far between.

My relationship with Michael began as a friendship based on deep trust. For me, trust is something that I have scarcely awarded. It has to be earned; you have to prove to me that you are worthy. That battle to prove oneself never happened here; I trusted him entirely from the start. The moment I looked into his eyes it was like I had always known him. I know it sounds cliche and I hate shit like that, but that's how it was. It was as if there was a level of recognition in my soul, a knowing him without ever having had met him before. It was almost like I could see his character, the strength of his soul, coming through those bright blue eyes. Anyone who knows him will tell you that he's soft-spoken, gentle, and kind, but he's also fucking hilarious and a lot of fun.

Our relationship wasn't an overnight thing. In the early days, Michael danced between interest and avoidance. Every time we paddled out to surf, I got to see him relaxed, in his element, with his guard down. Here, in the safety of the ocean, he would share pieces of his past with me, and I with him. I remember being shocked, impressed, and downright amazed that he is still alive. We learned about each other's pasts, how we came to be the people we are today, and rather than impose judgment on one another, we chose acceptance.

As our relationship transitioned, I learned that unconditional love was something Michael had never truly experienced, not from his family or from a significant other. His life was riddled with recurring acts of complex trauma that imprinted themselves during childhood, only to be revealed as an adult. There is a quote attributed to my favorite author, C. S. Lewis, that always stood out to me: "Love is never wasted, for its value does not rest upon reciprocity." Unconditional love was the only love I knew how to give, whether it be as a friend or a partner. I am not here to tell you how great of a partner I am; I am not perfect, and neither is Michael, but together we have created something that is perfect for us, a positive perfect storm if you will. I never set out with any intention of fixing Michael, nor am I telling you that he has been freed from the demons of his past. What has changed is that he was given the space to be himself, to be accepted for exactly who he is, and to receive encouragement to lean into that. It is said that if you love someone exactly as they are, you will see them flourish in all aspects of life. This I can say is true.

Over time, I have watched Michael begin to heal. It's a process and something we take on every day, but what I have seen is pretty remarkable. I can pinpoint the moment when things really began to shift. We were lying in bed, just about to fall asleep, when he told me that this was the safest place he had ever been, that what we had created together was the first time he felt like he could be exactly who he was. Michael had lived in a constant state of fight-or-flight from the moment he was born. When you think about what that does to someone's mind—the continual rush of adrenaline and cortisol, not to mention piling on multiple concussions and alcohol and drug use from a young age—his brain and body never had a chance to provide balance, to shift between sympathetic and parasympathetic nervous systems. There was no relaxation, no regulation, no rebuilding.

How can you sit down to write a book when you have spent your entire life in survival mode? When you are still in survival mode to this day? Easy, you can't—and thus began the journey of healing. Without creating a safe space for Michael's brain to rest, I don't think this story would have come to fruition. And trust me, that would be a damn shame. Michael's story is filled with raw honesty, addiction, and trauma responses expressed through romantic relationships. His story is also filled with incredible hope and a level of adventure that most of us only ever dream of. The ability to spend all you have left on a plane ticket, to embark on a journey of uncertainty, takes a level of bravery that I will forever be impressed with.

[PRESENT DAY]

Have you ever had a dream that, when you woke up, you swore was real? I laid in bed replaying every moment of that dream as if it were a movie.

~ ~ ~

River sees a package as she approaches the front door. It is wrapped in brown paper, the address handwritten with a return address in the United States. Her heart skips a beat; she immediately knows it's from her father, from me. She reaches for the package with both hands, a testament to how precious it is to her, and tucks it away into her backpack before heading inside.

She carries the package in her backpack the whole next day. The package, while light in weight, weighs heavily on her thoughts. She imagines her dad wrapping the brown paper, her mind focusing on his hands before moving up to his face. What does he look like? She can't remember exactly. She knows that she looks like him in every way—her mother has told her countless times.

River drifts in and out of thought, moving from lecture to lecture, half in, half out. School comes easily enough for her that she can zone out in the middle of a discussion and still be able to answer correctly if called on.

When the last bell has finally rung, River walks the long way home. She heads to her favorite spot, Kirra Hill Lookout, the spot she comes to when she needs to be alone, when she needs space to think. She sits at the top of the lookout, gazing out at the panoramic views of the Superbank. One of the longest right point breaks in the world. This hill is a hidden gem on the otherwise beautiful but busy Gold Coast. River watches the turquoise waves, cylinder in shape, marching down the point. Blues and greens spiraling together. This is one of River's favorite places in the world to surf, but not today. Today her mind is focused only on her father, on where he is, what he could have sent her, what he would think of her.

River looks over her shoulder to make sure she is alone. She unzips her backpack and slowly pulls out the package. She begins to open it, savoring every moment, letting her senses take over. She runs her fingers over the thick leather journal, feeling the indentations as though she is reading braille. A small piece of twine wrapped around holds a card. The envelope is off-white, thick, with a subtle texture that she thinks makes it feel more substantial than it is. She opens the envelope and takes a deep breath before beginning to read.

Dear River,

Happy 16th birthday, my beautiful girl. I can't believe you are already 16 and that it has been so long since I got to see you, to hold you, and to tell you that I love you. More than anything I need you to know that I have always, and will always, love you. I also want you to have a chance to get to know me and where I come from. This journal is a story of my life. The absolute highs and the lowest lows. It won't be easy to read at times, and for that I am sorry, but I owed it to you to be as honest as possible. I wish someone had done the same for me. These are the stories of my family...your family.

There are some things in this family that you might not know, from generational and childhood traumas to depression and addiction. I myself became an alcoholic early in life. I was just a teenager and ended up getting sober at the age of twenty-four. Crazy to think about now that I have been sober since that very day. Even crazier to think I became an alcoholic at all, after swearing that I would never become such a thing after experiencing what my father, your grandpa, went through and, in turn, what he put us through. It didn't stop there. Even after getting sober, it was one addiction after another, in sobriety. You name it, and I've been addicted to it. Come to find out this was just a way of coping with never feeling safe in the world. When I found something that felt good, I rode it hard and did it as often as possible to escape the turmoil that I was feeling inside every day.

Beyond addiction, I struggled with self-sabotage, which has been the most painful part of my journey, mostly because it is how I lost you. For a long time, I hated how bad my life was, but at the same time, I wasn't okay with life being good. Sounds crazy, I know. Maybe you can relate, although I hope not. Things were so tumultuous for me as a kid that high-stress situations felt normal and somehow even felt good to me. Because of this, I felt numb in situations that were filled with peace, calm, and love. There is a lot of science behind this, but I won't bore you with it here. I am sure you already know a lot about this because you are so smart and you always have been. At a very young age, you were already putting full sentences together. I remember being in awe of you.

Call it PTSD if you will, but I was so used to being in a state of survival from the time I was a kid that I constantly leaned on things outside of myself to provide some sort of escape or comfort.

Through trial and error, I figured this out the hard way, and one of the most important things I've learned is to not become "the victim" but to take responsibility for my life and heal. My hope is that you never face the demons that I did, but if you do, maybe my story can be a guide for you. If not, take what you like and leave the rest, my dear.

Please know that while I have had some downs, I have also had some of the most incredible experiences life can offer. I have come to learn that life is a balance of the yin and yang perpetually leveling out. I have traveled the world, met some remarkable people, and in that journey I had you. I am grateful every day that you are in this world. I was so excited to be your father when you were in your mother's belly. I had so many fun adventures planned for us. I wanted to be the best dad... **Your** dad. Life sure turned out a lot different than I had planned. One of my all-time favorite quotes is from John Lennon's song "Beautiful Boy," when he sings about life happening when you're focused on other plans. It couldn't be truer for me. I'm so sorry for the way things turned out.

How do you drop a plate on the floor, break it into a hundred pieces, then say you're sorry? You can't.

It won't change anything. It's broken, and I know that.

I know that I can't change the past, but I want you to know that I am here for you, that I am honored to call you my daughter. I hope that there is time for us, for me, to be your dad. I can't think of anything more I would like in this world than to get to have a relationship with you. I understand if that isn't something you are interested in, but I am here if, and when, that ever changes.

Either way, I will love you, always.

Your father,

Mike

Her chestnut eyes well up with tears. River does nothing to hold them back, letting them mix with the mist of the ocean, soaking her cheeks. She is in a trance, mindlessly watching the waves roll in and crash along the reef. All her life she has wondered about her father. Mostly if he ever wanted her but also why he stayed away all this time.

River can't bring herself to open the journal on the beach; she is in too much shock, too lost in thought to be able to process anything.

Two days pass before River retreats to her room early, telling her mom she has a ton of homework. She closes her door, takes a deep breath, and discreetly locks the door, ensuring that she doesn't make a sound. If her mom comes around, she will think of something to say, but at least she will have a chance to hide the journal first. It's not that she has anything to hide; she just wants to read in privacy.

River unfolds the pages of the letter. She slowly reads each word as if it were the first time.

She runs her fingers along the last line, *Your father, Mike.*

With care, River opens the front cover and begins to read...

[SOLANA BEACH, CA —JUNE 2006]

I'll never forget the night my dad started drinking again. It had been fifteen years since he had last picked up the bottle; that bottle which time after time turned him into a destructive and malicious beast. I had never seen him this way, but heard the stories from my mom and even my dad.

I was lying in bed, somewhere between awake and asleep, between alive and dead. The curtains were drawn, making it hard to tell if it was morning or night. I had never imagined that this was what twenty would feel like. That this was what would become of me, and that the overwhelming feeling of anguish I had felt for so many years would completely swallow me.

The room was cold, and I felt a sense of terror. I wondered if I was still drunk or if the ecstasy I had taken last night had poison in it or was just cut with bad speed. *Wouldn't it be easier if I were dead?* I thought to myself, feeling like I was dying.

The phone rang. I watched *Mom* flash on the screen for a few moments before I decided to pick up.

Doing the best I could to sound coherent, "Hi Mom, what's up?"

My mom struggled to control her sobbing. "Michael, I'm sorry to call you like this. Your dad is drinking. He just finished a bottle of rum and left the house. Can you please get here as soon as possible?"

I jolted out of bed, immediately more sober. I had a deep knot in my stomach. It was feelings of fear and discomfort that I was used to, but this was a new level of it. I had grown accustomed to instability and periods of sheer chaos, but that was when he was sober. It had been so long since my dad was drunk that I had no idea what to expect.

I began to put some clothes on. "Shit, Mom, okay, I'll come right now."

I hopped in my black single-cab '97 Toyota pickup truck and started to make my way to my parents' house. They had been lucky enough to land an apartment in a senior citizen complex after being homeless for a period of time. Just as I was arriving, I saw my dad driving off in his '65 Chrysler New Yorker, more of a boat than a car. I watched him swerve around the road, thinking to myself that he was obviously drunk and that this wasn't gonna end well.

I couldn't handle this on my own. I needed Mark's help.

My cousin, Mark, was like a younger brother to me. He was a pain in the ass. I loved him and hated him more than anyone on the planet. He was a talent freak and a daredevil—zero fear. It was more than being fearless, though; he had a death wish. He was almost always funny and a good time, but there was a side of him that loved trouble. He was an instigator and a rebel. He did everything I did, and did it better. He was there for everything—all of the good and all of the bad, and trust me, the bad outweighed the good. We had to stick together because neither of us really had parents. I mean, we had parents who were physically alive, but from the time we were young, it was more like we were parenting them.

"Yo?" Mark said, as if he was surprised to see me calling him.

"Mark, my dad is fucking hammered and driving the Chrysler. I'm following him, and I need backup. I'll let you know where we end up, but man, I really need you."

"Holy shit are you serious? What a fuckin' idiot. Okay, let me know."

Following my dad through our neighborhood, we passed by million-dollar homes with perfect lawns and even more perfect families inside, or so I thought at the time. *God sure is a sick bastard,* I thought to myself, *forcing me to grow up in poverty surrounded by ultra-wealthy, spoiled pieces of shit.* When I say poverty, I mean I grew up on food stamps, couch surfing all over the nation, staying with my mom's family or friends. For a period of time, we even lived in the back of my dad's mattress store, which looked more like a thrift store than your typical mattress store. My parents, whether they were together or separated, couldn't seem to keep a roof over our heads.

I definitely had a chip on my shoulder, and to be completely honest, I still do. I'm nowhere near as bad as I used to be, because I've learned that judging my insides with other peoples' outside is never accurate. Some of the most miserable people I have ever met, with the most terrifying problems, also happen to be the wealthiest people I have ever met. They appear to have lives filled with excitement, abundance, travel, and creativity, with Instagram accounts that make you so jealous that you want to neck yourself. In reality, a lot of times these people are some of the most negative, depressed, and sometimes even suicidal people I have ever encountered.

I continued to follow my dad down the hill toward the coast, the road illuminated by dim streetlights.

My dad parked near a cliff overlooking our local surf break, Pillbox. The break earned its name from the old World War II military lookout point, which resembles a pillbox and is accompanied by an old communist-era-looking community center. Its appearance was yet another contrast to the surrounding homes. It is where I learned to surf, my dad taking me out on a 1970s short board when I was ten years old. Over the years I'd surf here with my dad, Mark, and all of our buddies every day after school.

I kept driving down the residential street. My dad was too drunk to notice that I was following him. Eventually, I pulled to the side to park. I was far enough away to observe him from a distance. I watched my dad stumble toward the cliff and lean on the barrier fence.

He paused.

Looked down, mumbling to himself on the edge of a two-hundred-foot drop.

I immediately knew that this was bad. That this time was different. Up until this point, I had only seen my dad drink once before. Sure, he was a loose cannon, but he had always been someone I could count on. Being with him might not have been perfect but it was the most stable existence I knew. Watching my dad drunk, standing on the edge of a cliff, put all of that in jeopardy. Quickly, I called Mark to let him know where we were before getting out of the car.

Sliding out of my seat, I emerged from the car. I quietly and gently closed the door, doing the best I could not to make a sound. I began to approach my dad with caution, worried, scared, but also doing my best to stay calm. Over the years, I had grown accustomed to a high-stress life. I had lived in a perpetual state of fight-or-flight most of my life, and that calmness is a badge of all the years of survival.

I saw my dad standing there on the edge of the cliff. The moon illuminated his big red face, making it look pale and giving it a blue-gray appearance. In the midst of all the fear, I remember thinking that the shorts he was wearing were ridiculous, that they were too short for the current time period: OP corduroy shorts, artifacts of the '80s.

Turning back, my dad's gaze landed in my direction. He squinted his eyes in the dark to try and make out who was coming his way.

"Dad," I said, realizing he was so drunk that he wasn't sure it was me.

"Mikey? Whatta you doing here...how did you..."

"Mom called me and told me you pounded a bottle of rum."

Drunk, sad, almost confused, "Oh did she..." he trailed off as he saw the lights of Mark's beat-up 1990 Honda Accord approaching.

Mark parked and began to walk over. His sharp features echoed by his even sharper bite as his stocky five-foot-ten frame perfectly displayed just how annoyed and scared he was. Mark really was an aggressive, shit-talking, smart-ass who would either be super helpful or create a lot of havoc, depending on the situation. I was really hoping for helpful here, but it was obvious from the way he walked over to us that he held a deep resentment, maybe even hatred, for his Uncle Nicholas.

"Oh, Mark's here too, huh?"

"Yeah, Dad, we came here to check on you and make sure you were alright."

"I'm all fucked up, kid," he said, sobbing in self-pity. "I failed you, I'm sorry."

Taken aback and nervous, I quickly told him, "No, Dad, you didn't fail me. I have a good life. I love you."

My dad continued to sob deeply. "No, I fucked up. I'm sorry I wasn't able to take care of you or send you to college. I'm a failure. I don't wanna live anymore!!"

"Whatta you mean, Dad?" I asked, doing what I could to keep him talking in the hopes I could calm him down.

My dad started motioning like he was going to jump off the cliff. Mark and I were positioned on each side of him, grabbing him by the arms, holding him back. He was pretty brittle from all the drinking, but he definitely would have jumped if we hadn't been there. I watched the pebbles slide off the edge into the abyss. Everything after that is a blur of shouting and tears.

I remember thinking that the closest thing I had to a rock in this world wanted to leave this life. There are no words to describe what that feels like. There was a girl in my high school whose mom had committed suicide a year prior. I didn't even know her that well, but I still felt such deep pain for her. Now I was close to standing in her shoes.

It might be hard to believe, but not too long before this moment, my dad had fifteen years of sobriety. Whether it was surfing or taking us on adventures, he was experiencing moments of joy being my dad; I saw it with my own eyes. What I didn't see my dad doing was taking his sobriety seriously. I'm talking about going to AA meetings consistently. I never saw him go through the Twelve Steps with a sponsor, never saw him help another alcoholic. Not that I knew what those things were back then, but I do now. It is said that you can't keep the gift of sobriety unless you give it away. All of these things are critical for a person who is in recovery. It helps you stay out of your own way. It brings a level of awareness and humility that you simply wouldn't achieve on your own. Again, trust me. I've tried. Alcoholics are some of the most self-absorbed people on the planet, and usually blind to it. So when I say he had fifteen years of sobriety, what I mean is that he was a dry drunk who was white-knuckling the whole process.

My dad used other addictions while "sober" to numb his pain. Gambling, sex, nicotine, Diet Coke, violence...he did all of these alcoholically. He was constantly hiding things. Things like stopping at the pharmacy in Tijuana to get Valium on our way to go on a fishing and prostitute run in Ensenada. That's not sober behavior.

I remember being ten years old, riding in the truck with him on one particular occasion. Everything was going great on the drive down together. It was just him and I and I was always so excited to go out fishing on a cattle boat in Mexico. We would chat and laugh about things on the way down, my dad reaching over to pinch my left ear. He was always pinching my ears. His jaw clenching as he gripped the steering wheel with the other hand, externalizing his constant stress, imprinting it on to me. We stopped at the pharmacy in Tijuana; I didn't know why, but I didn't ask. Sometime during the next hour of the drive from the border, to Ensenada, the pills must have started to kick in, and my dad became a different person.

Everything went silent and still.

It was like a demon had slipped into the cab of the truck, and I was sitting next to a complete stranger. It wasn't my dad, and it terrified me. I remember being so scared that I didn't say a word that night. We made it to Ensenada, checked into the room, and went to sleep.

Growing up in this environment was uncomfortable, to say the least, but it got much worse when he relapsed and started drinking again. After holding my dad back, Mark and I carried him back to my car. We sat him up in between the two of us and drove him to the small apartment he shared with my mom. My mom was rattled but she helped us get him into bed. As crazy as this night was, the crazier thing is that things got so bad for my parents after this that we never spoke about this moment again.

It's still hard to believe that after that evening, my dad lost everything—again—and in turn gained the qualities of a monster. He became a loud, rude, and violent man who was scary to be around. Top that off with the massive amounts of false pride, ego, and racist tendencies, and it put the fear of God in me.

I remember thinking that for my whole life, up until that point, we were always fighting to get to a better place, to have a home, to be a family. There were moments where it seemed like it was possible, like it was happening, but in that moment that idea was crushed. Not only did things not get better but it felt like the worst possible outcome came true. I never in a million years thought that things could get worse. All that hope I had that things would get better and that we would somehow become a strong family...all that was gone.

[SOLANA BEACH, CA —2004]

It wasn't always like this for me. I wasn't always this idiot who was hiding from the world. I honestly don't even know how I got there.

I think back to when I was sixteen years old, to when I truly fell in love with surfing and dedicated myself to it. I spent every moment I could out in the water, and it was paying off.

People have no clue how hard surfing is. They think they are going to show up and just start ripping. Yeah, good luck. This is because surfers make it look so easy. It takes a lifetime to get good at surfing. If you don't start before the age of fifteen, it's almost impossible to reach a certain level. And fifteen is late. Sure, you can start surfing at any age and have a lot of fun, and I encourage all who have the opportunity to do so. Surfing has the power to change lives. But go easy on yourself. It's said that surfing has the slowest learning curve of any sport.

The most arduous part of surfing is gaining ocean knowledge. I usually tell people who are starting from scratch that they need to surf a minimum of two to three times per week for at least six months straight, and then they might start seeing some progress. People with a background in yoga, gymnastics, or dance usually progress more quickly. Sure, you can have someone push you into a wave and you stand up and ride for a time, but that's cheating. I'm talking about actually paddling out, through the impact zone, into the lineup, turning around, and paddling into a wave on your own steam.

There are so many different variables that go into surfing. Everything from the different types of breaks to wind, swell, and tide conditions impacts how the waves behave—and how you interact with them. Whether it be a beach break, reef break, point break, slab, novelty wave, cobblestone wave, longboard wave, sharky wave, etc.—they all require a different approach.

There are many different types of reefs as well. Razor-sharp coral reef, mossy reef, urchin-covered reefs, dead reef, and so on. Some reef waves behave like sandbar waves, and there are sandbar waves that behave like reef waves.

There are different types of swell generated from different types of storms. Ground swells come from massive storms that are really far away. These are usually the best because they have a lot of power and they've covered a lot of distance, becoming more groomed and organized over time before they hit a location. Wind swells can be great as well, but they are usually from storms that are closer and haven't had as much time to organize themselves. Ground swells have a longer period in between waves, while wind swells have a shorter period.

Whenever I take someone new to surfing out in the water, they constantly ask me how I know which waves are good. I tell them it's like learning how to read. How do you explain learning to read to someone? You can't do it all in one session. They have to learn, and it takes time. Learning to read waves is harder than actually learning how to read written words. Over time, you're able to gain a better understanding of how the ocean works and become in tune with it.

It's spiritual, in a sense. I've gone through periods when I am living in tune with life around me, and the ocean rewards me. I've also gone through periods where I am living selfishly and the ocean sends me straight onto the reef. If it's a coral reef, it's like landing on a cheese grater on the whole side of my body, ending up completely covered in blood. Some of the top surfers in the world have a deep connection with the ocean. It seems that the ocean magically produces waves for them. It's a very impressive thing to see.

I learned early on that all my problems dissolved when I was in the water. It was medicine for me, my antidepressant. It was being on land that was the problem. Every time you go into the water it is an energetic cleanse; everything that's weighing on you on land lifts. The majority of the time you come out from the water with a clearer perspective, as if the things you were stressing about aren't as important as you thought they were.

If you've never surfed or spent time around the ocean, you probably have no idea what I'm talking about. And this is what I mean. It takes years to learn all this, but it is such a fun process and the best feeling in the world when you score.

From the moment I was hooked on surfing, my heroes became Bruce and Andy Irons, Rob Machado, and Kelly Slater. I saw them in magazines, videos, and in real life. Bruce and Andy happened to be from Kauai, so I would see them around; they'd even stop by my uncle's house when I was living out there when I was fourteen.

A couple of years later, when I moved back to California, I started surfing a well-known spot called Seaside in San Diego. There I would see Rob Machado surfing in person almost every day. These guys were larger than life to me. Since I was young and impressionable, they seemed to have the best lives imaginable. They surfed every day, traveled the globe, partied their asses off, and got paid to do it.

There was also something special about seeing them in person that you don't get to see through magazines and videos. They had a special aura about them—like gods in a way—and I idolized them. I know calling them gods might seem like a bit much, but if you think about how different their lives are compared to the average person, it's hard to deny how blessed they are.

More than any other surfer, Andy Irons was my ultimate hero. I related to him so much, especially the part about having a younger brother who, some might say, was more naturally talented and better looking. It was similar to what my cousin Mark was to me. When they were younger, Bruce got all of the attention of the surfing world. He was considered the best free surfer in the world, and he was, in my opinion, the most photogenic surfer of all time. The absolute best style, always making the ultra-difficult look easy. Bruce was constantly landing all the best video parts, magazine covers, and spreads.

While Bruce was gaining public recognition, somehow in the background, Andy kept grinding on the World Tour. He was known as a bit of a loose cannon and a party animal, but then he made some big changes and became hyper-focused on the World Tour. Here was a guy who, against all odds, took the surfing world by storm. He went on to win three consecutive world titles in a row, and in the process, gave eleven-time world champion, Kelly Slater, the biggest rivalry of his career.

Andy Irons was one of those guys who was either going to win the contest or lose the first heat. You never knew what you were going to get. So raw and unpredictable...so human. I, like many others, loved him for that. I was rooting for him in every contest and webcast I watched.

Andy Irons' story ended tragically, in one of the saddest ways humanly possible. His wife was pregnant with their first child and Andy was headed back from a contest in Puerto Rico. During his layover in Texas, he passed away in his sleep from a drug overdose. It ripped out the hearts of the surfing world. And, by the way, when I say he was my hero, I mean that I was doing everything to model his behavior.

I was winning amateur contests and getting exposure in magazines. A couple of years earlier this would have seemed unheard of for me because I was such a late bloomer in the surf world. While most kids were focused on competing at a very young age, I was being dragged around the country with my mom. I went to eight different school districts in twelve years. Things were finally grounded enough for me to focus on surfing when I was sixteen. After coming back from Kauai, I lived with my dad. He put me to work at his mattress store making deliveries and working as a salesman on the floor. My dad was doing his best to make a comeback after having had multiple successful business ventures in the past. I was able to earn enough money to afford buying surfboards consistently (they have a tendency to break easily) and spent all my free time surfing. On paper, we were living below the poverty line, but we weren't on food stamps the way I was with my mom, which was a huge relief. Not having to wonder if we would make rent or have food allowed me to spend every extra minute of the day on surfing. I'm not acting like I was better than I was: I failed miserably as a pro-surfer, but to be successful, it usually takes a kid who is not just on fire for surfing but who also has strong family and financial support. Someone with the right backing, who knows where that kid could take his surfing. Almost all people who do well in surfing these days were born and bred to do it. They had a soccer mom or dad who would fund the whole process, taking them to every competition. It takes a lot of time, money, and emotional support from your family.

I had none of these things; in fact, I had the exact opposite. If I came home with a trophy after winning a contest and was all excited to show my dad, he might be excited and say, "Wow, great job, son," but then down the line somewhere he would say things like, "You know what, kid, I really hope this doesn't ruin your life." On the other hand, I would hear stories of my dad going around town showing people my photos in magazines and they would always go on about how proud he was of me. I guess he couldn't show it.

~ ~ ~

A big part of my drive to succeed was that I desperately wanted to make my mom proud, whether I lived with her or not, and to distract her from her cancer diagnosis. I know now that she never even had cancer; she just made it up to hide the fact that she might have hepatitis C. To be fair, she only told me about having cancer because she didn't think it was appropriate to tell her son that she potentially contracted something that he wouldn't understand. In the end, she didn't have hepatitis C either.

I really thought that I could make things better for her. I thought that if I became a successful surfer, she would be happy. I can't tell you how much drive this gave me. I did everything for her.

It was hard for me to come to terms with the fact that my mom never seemed too impressed with my surfing. But on one occasion, soon after she moved back in with my dad and I, I did see a brief glimpse of happiness in her when I landed a full-page ad in a mainstream surf magazine.

We were driving down the Pacific Coast Highway in my mom's 1989 Pontiac Grand Prix. She had just graduated from cosmetology school and was feeling quite accomplished. It was the accomplishment she was the most proud of. SweetPea, her chihuahua-wiener dog, was in the car with us. SweetPea was usually by her side—she was her emotional support dog, and you could tell by the way my mom constantly rubbed and pinched her ears.

Sitting in the passenger seat, I saw *Unknown Number* come up across the screen of my flip phone. I answered, "Hello?"

A bubbly voice responded, "Hi, is this Mike?"

"Yes, it is."

"Good! My name is Ellie from AC Clothing, and I'm calling to let you know we're planning on running a full-page ad of you in *Surfing Magazine*."

Ellie sounded exactly like you'd imagine. Early thirties,

California surfer girl who got stuck in an office. She had bleached blonde hair and tan skin to match.

Shocked, I responded, "What?! No way."

"We just need you to come in and sign some paperwork."

"Okay, sounds good."

"Does Tuesday at 1:00 p.m. work for you?" she asked.

"Yeah! Thanks so much!"

"Absolutely. Okay, see you Tuesday."

Hanging up the phone, unable to contain my excitement, I said, "Mom, I'm getting an ad in *Surfing Magazine*!"

"Oh wow! That's awesome, Michael. Congratulations! That's so exciting!"

"What the hell?" I said, completely stunned, with a huge smile across my face.

We spent the rest of the drive keeping to ourselves. My mom singing along with the radio, and me staring out the window toward the ocean, just watching the waves come in, thinking there's no better feeling in the world. For a young person, especially one who has experienced a lot of turmoil, recognition can be really important. That need for validation is constantly present, and it's not always healthy. In this moment, I started to feel like I was on a path to fame—like success was possible.

[DEL MAR, CA —OCTOBER 2001]

My mom moved us around constantly. As a result, I went to a lot of different schools.

I started high school in Kauai and spent my freshman and sophomore years there. It was tough. Growing up, the level of hate toward white people in Hawaii was insane. If you have grown up in or spent time in Hawaii, you know. It's definitely still there; maybe not quite as bad, but it's there. It's a full-on role reversal from the mainland. The minorities have the upper hand. The older local kids look for any excuse to beat up haoles (pronounced hau-lees), otherwise known as white kids. I am part indigenous and had cousins who were born and raised there, so I was able to slide under the radar most of the time, but that doesn't mean I came out totally unscathed. I went through my fair share of hate—as did every white kid.

I hated going to school there. I was always scared that someone was gonna fuck with me. And they did. I handled it for as long as I could. Slowly but surely, I started going to school less and less. My house was right above the high school. I would skate right past it in the morning, my surfboard tucked under my arm, and head straight down to the beach. I started hitchhiking around the island.

I was staying away from booze, but I was smoking weed every day. It's just something you do in Hawaii. If you don't, you're considered a pussy. At one point I started getting into growing weed and I hadn't gone to school for six months straight. This is a fast track to a drug dealer life and jail time for many in Hawaii. My mom could see where things were going and decided it would be best to put me on a plane back to live with my dad in California again to straighten me up. I didn't put up much of a fight.

~ ~ ~

When I got back to California, I was certain that I would be held back a year, but they let me do summer school, and I got all caught up and stayed in my class. Well below average but still in the same grade. My family never had a computer, so I didn't know how to type. I managed to complete my work without one since my upbringing taught me to be resourceful. Back in California, I perfected the balance of knowing, and being cool with the bullies, but I am also a dork at heart, so I always related to, and had friends who were, nerds. When a paper was due, I would write it out by hand, then get one of my fast-typing nerd friends to complete the final copy. Throughout high school, most of my friends were surfers. When I was younger, it was more of a mix with a good amount of my friends being jocks. My jock days ended when I fell in love with surfing—when I learned that the ocean was the safest place in the world for me.

When my junior year started, I was reunited with all my friends from middle school. It felt great to be back, and it was as if no time had passed between us. We had one new addition, though. Ari became one of my closest friends and was the kid who would unknowingly have one of the biggest impacts on my sobriety.

Ari had just shown up from Bali. He looked like a surfer, and he managed to pick my friend Brett out of the crowd, knowing by the look of him that he was a fellow surfer. The two of them really looked the part, towhead blonde kids with permanent tans. New or not, Ari had no fear in going right up to Brett and asking him if he surfed. That was it; that was how Ari got introduced to us. We had a bench at school that was dedicated to our crew, known as the "surfers' bench." Ari hung there every day from that moment on.

Ari was an old soul. It was more than that unmistakable quality that comes from growing up abroad. He was more comfortable with older people, he didn't hang out with anyone his age, and he had a kindness and a level of maturity that you really only find in those who have had a different upbringing than those from the States. All of this was offset by his really funny, twangy accent. It was a mix of American, Indonesian, Australian, and European, which is the typical accent for first-generation children of expats in Bali.

He started to hang and surf with us, integrating himself into our crew instantly. We had a lot of good times together and came to know him as this bubbly, super-friendly kid who was always cracking jokes. Ari was a complete straight edge. I was obsessed with this kid because he was from Bali, and it was always my dream to be able to go to a place like that. As much as I wanted to go, I never thought I would be able to afford a trip to Bali—or anywhere else, really.

At some point, while we were still in high school, Ari decided to smoke weed for the first time. The moment he did, everything changed. Something shifted in him. It's crazy. People always hear about weed being a gateway drug and they think it's ridiculous or laugh it off, believing it to be harmless, but for some people who are wired a bit differently, and definitely with Ari, it truly was his entry point to drugs. He was one of those people who started and never stopped, and it completely changed his personality. All he wanted to do was seek out drugs and drink. He was completely obsessed with it.

Over the years, Ari would go back and forth between California and Bali. When he was in California, he tried going to school in Santa Barbara for a period of time. It didn't stick. He was getting in a lot of trouble and was constantly in and out of rehabs.

Every time I saw him, all he wanted to talk about was drug stories. It got to a point that we sort of coined a new term for him. Whenever Ari would start up a new drug story, my friends and I would be like, "Ooo drug stories, drug stories. Oh here we go, drug stories, drug stories." It became really annoying.

I remember asking him, "Hey man, don't you wanna maybe go surf? Or do some stuff that we used to do? Don't you want to just go have some fun?"

He never changed. He never came back to being the innocent kid from Bali that I knew.

[PERU —JULY 2004]

The year after I graduated from high school, I got a chance to go surfing in Peru. Mark was headed there with one of our high school heroes, Mason. This guy was a couple of years older than us and one of the best surfers in our hometown. He surfed like Rob Machado and was one of the nicest, humblest people you'd ever meet. Things were challenging for me at home, my parents' lives were tanking, and I jumped at the chance to join them on this trip. I remember thinking *fuck it*, we were focused on our surf careers and were looking to spend a month in Peru's world-famous hollow lefts honing our tube-riding skills. Mark and I had some friends from Peru who were going to college in San Diego, and our plan was to stay with them while they were back home for the summer.

We scraped our pennies together, and the three of us landed in Lima. I was nineteen years old. Peru felt unsafe as soon as we landed at the airport. It had an overwhelming feeling of struggle that is unique to a Third World country—corruption mixed with heavy security but also the possibility of being able to get away with whatever you want as long as you have enough money to buy your way out. Our good friend Poto picked us up at the airport and took us to his family's home. We didn't know it at the time, but we came to find out that Poto was from an ultra-wealthy family that was heavily involved in the tobacco business. Their home was nice, but what threw me was the heavy security all around it. Poto was a professional surfer and had this whole Prince of Lima thing going on. It's funny meeting surfers from around the world. More often than not, if they're from a Third World country, you can almost guarantee that they come from a wealthy family. It's a few rich and many poor in countries like that. Only wealthy kids can afford the equipment or have the time to get out and surf.

We dropped our stuff at the house, jumped in Poto's Audi sports car, and went for a spin around Lima. I've never been so scared being in a car in my life. It felt like he was going one hundred miles per hour on small streets, dipping in and out of lanes, going up on sidewalks, just barely missing pedestrians, and he was doing it all with a chuckle and a great big evil grin.

We spent a couple of days with Poto before linking up with our other friend Ricardo. He knew we were in town and invited us to stay with him and join him on the drive down to this famous surf city called Mancora, near the border of Ecuador. We made our way from the polluted waters off the coast of Lima, checking out nightlife and eating chifa. Chifa is a Chinese and Peruvian fusion of food. Come to find out there was a large population of Chinese people in Lima. If you can imagine a mix of Asian and Spanish food, you're getting kind of close. It was delicious. Just one of those things that you would have no idea existed unless you were there in the flesh.

Our plan was to surf the entire coast on the way to Mancora. The longest left in the world, called Chicama, is in Peru and we were so excited to surf it—that is, until we found out that it was a pretty weak wave that didn't offer any barrel sections. The drive up was sketchy. Ricardo and his friends had countless horror stories for us of abductions, murders, and so on. We drove through stretches of desert that felt like they lasted hundreds of miles without seeing anything. I remember seeing trash flowing through the desert with no one around. It was a disheartening sight. When you have friends from a Third World country, you skip the tourist parts. You get to see another side of the country and another side of your friends that you really don't see when they are in the States. For example, in California, we're not used to growing up around guns. At one point, Ricardo pulled over in the middle of the desert and pulled out a gun that none of us knew he had. There was really no reason for it, but he just started unloading rounds into the endless desert.

We didn't score any great waves on the drive up. We surfed a couple of times, just to get wet, but nothing to write home about. When we arrived in Mancora, the waves were flat, and it happened to be Peru's Independence Day. The otherwise quiet little town turned into a party epicenter.

We were all exhausted and took a nap when we arrived. When we woke up, we noticed that Mark and Ricardo were gone. When Mark came back, he was a bit rattled and confused, but excited. He was only seventeen at the time, and apparently, Ricardo and all his friends circled Mark and made him take an ecstasy pill. This would've been his first time. At this point, all of us were relatively clean kids. Neither Mason nor I had ever tried ecstasy, and to be honest I never really wanted to. I wasn't into trying anything hard; all I wanted to do was surf. For some reason, after we heard what happened to Mark, we decided we all better stick together, and we would do it with him. We hopped from bar to bar, drinking and feeling fucking amazing. Ecstasy really does make you feel amazing. You feel goooood. You have a warmth and bliss in your chest. I don't know how else to put it—you feel ecstasy. As the sun was coming up, we all made it back to the room relatively safe and passed out.

In the coming days, the swell picked up, and we got incredible left point breaks up and down the coast around Mancora. Ricardo and his friends were a bit older than us, and all they wanted to do was drink and party, a lot. All we wanted to do was surf. We were there to train, hone our skills, and have fun. We ended up renting a shack in the middle of nowhere near a left point break. Just the three of us surfing a mostly empty left. We would take breaks from surfing to film each other from the beach. Those are moments in time that I will never forget.

After a couple of weeks in northern Peru, Ricardo picked us up, and we began making the trek back down south toward Lima. We'd just had the best surf trip of our lives. We were pretty excited about the footage we got along Peru's surf-rich coast. Toward the end of our trip, our footage mysteriously went missing. We later came to the conclusion that Ricardo stole the footage, either because he wanted the few clips that he had on the camera, or he didn't want us exposing the local surf spots in Peru. Either way, we were pissed and honestly sad about it. Even though he never admitted it, we knew he took it. I don't know how people can smile to your face and then steal behind your back, especially when they are supposed to be your friend.

[NORTH COUNTY SAN DIEGO, CA —SEPTEMBER 2005]

My first summer as an ocean lifeguard in North County San Diego came to a close in a way I never imagined. Overall, I really enjoyed my first season as a lifeguard. It came fairly naturally to me after so many years of surfing. While most strong pool swimmers mainly used a buoy and fins to make a rescue, I used the rescue board. I was able to paddle up to someone in distress, put them in front of me on the rescue board, and paddle them to the shore. If you grew up around the ocean, it's not a big deal to swim back to the beach if you get stuck in a current, but for so many, they don't know what to do. It's a pretty incredible feeling to save someone's life who has no idea how the ocean works. If you're from Arizona, for example, and have zero ocean knowledge, a slight current could pull you out to sea, and that's the end of it. I've seen it happen.

It happened just like they said it would in the academy, right at the end of my first season on Labor Day weekend. The beach was packed. It was toward the end of my shift, around 3:30 in the afternoon. We had a relatively big south swell in the water. It was a negative low tide, which tends to spread everything out as far as surfing and people go. There were hundreds of people scattered out along the shore and in the water.

I was alone in the tower, the afternoon sun blazing straight into my eyes even with sunglasses on, as I scanned the lineup. As a lifeguard, you are never allowed to take your eye off the ocean or have your back to the water. Out of nowhere, a young girl comes running up to the right side of my tower screaming that somebody has drowned in the water.

The protocol for something like this is to pick up the phone in the tower and throw it off the hook, allowing you to pursue the person in trouble as soon as possible, ultimately increasing their chances of survival. By throwing the phone off the hook, my superiors know there is an emergency and that they should get help to the tower as soon as possible. I ran about 2,00 yards north of the tower as fast as I could, scanning the lineup. As I ran into the ocean, I could see surfers holding on to the person who had drowned. I got to them as soon as possible, running through the shallow water before duck-diving the rest of the way.

When I arrived, the two teenage boys were shouting for help and crying. The man was in his late fifties/early sixties and was completely unconscious. I held him the way I was trained to in my academy and first-responder courses, getting behind him, looping my arms under his shoulders, and bracing his neck to keep it as straight as possible in case of spinal damage. At this time, I was around twenty years old and weighed about 145 pounds. This man was over six feet tall, and roughly 220 to 230 pounds. It was exhausting bringing him in. In Lifeguard Academy, we were taught to get the individual to the beach as soon as possible to start resuscitation. Trying to resuscitate someone in the water without a solid foundation underneath them is basically pointless.

"Do something, do something!" the boys screamed as I was bringing the man to the shore. I'd come to find out they were his sons. Everything registered for them as I told them I needed to get him back to the shore as soon as possible. The man had dived headfirst into a rock while surfing, snapping his neck instantly. I could see blood on his forehead from the impact and blood coming out of his mouth. As I got to the shore, my superiors were there to take over. The man's wife and sons stood by in absolute terror, the wife bawling her eyes out the entire time.

There on the beach, they were able to resuscitate him. A helicopter landed on the sand to evac him out. We later found out that the man was told he was going to be paralyzed and on life support. By communicating through blinking his eyes, he asked to be taken off life support, saying goodbye to his family in the way that he could, passing away shortly after.

Back at our headquarters, the team held a debriefing. The whole unit was there. It all was a bit of a blur to me. I got called on to share by my superiors. I can't even remember what I said. I remember being embarrassed that I shed some tears. In the moment, I wasn't sure whether or not I did a good job. I felt horrible for the mother and two sons. One minute this father and his sons were surfing together and having a great time, while his wife was sunbathing on the beach; the next he was gone. I couldn't get the feeling of holding his lifeless neck out of my head. It felt limp, and I could hear cracking as I was making my way to the shore.

The captain, lieutenant, and sergeant all made sure that I

knew that my response was normal and that I did an outstanding job. Later that season I received the Rookie of the Year award. It was an amazing feeling to be rewarded, but I would give it all back in a second for that family to be whole again.

[PECHANGA CASINO, CA —MARCH 2006]

Alcohol wasn't my dad's only addiction, and maybe not even the hardest one for him to come to terms with. Despite being homeless, my dad gambled so frequently that the casino would offer him a free room once in a while. My parents would use that as a reprieve from living in their car, taking the opportunity to sleep in a real bed, rest, shower, and play penny slots.

Truth be told, my parents had it rough.

My dad had recently been forced to close his mattress store of ten years after a series of bad blows. After a lifetime of carrying furniture, he blew out a disc in his back, forcing him to need back surgery. The doctor put him on Vicodin. In their defense, he never mentioned to the doctor that he was in recovery. The pills became another form of escape, another addiction—which led him back to alcohol. To make matters worse, the building where he had the mattress store was bought out by this Arab guy. According to my dad, he said he was going to partner with him, but instead, he raised the rent and pushed him out. "Fucking camel jockeys backstabbed me, son," he would say.

When I went to see them at the casino, my parents had just gotten back from staying with my mom's family in Hawaii for the past six months. They went out there when my dad lost the store, which was also where they happened to be living. I hadn't seen them for a while, so I went to the casino to see how they were doing. I made my way through the depressing casino floor on the way to my parents' room. It was filled with elderly people who seemed as though they had collectively decided to give up on life and fair play because they'd all be dead soon. The only excitement they seemed to get was in gambling the last of their money in the hopes of hitting it big. They would sit there all day, in the air-conditioned rooms, pets on their laps, ordering Diet Cokes and eating tasty five-dollar steaks for dinner. The casinos find a way to make it all sustainable.

I knocked on the door. My dad swung it open, already turning back to the TV, making sure he didn't miss a moment of the game. I watched him take a swig of beer. Fifteen years of his version of sobriety down the drain. A deep, painful feeling of fear began to boil up in me. I had heard countless stories about his drinking in the past, but before this moment, I had never seen my dad drink. To say alarms were going off was an understatement.

"How's it going, Dad?" I asked, almost nervously.

"Oh, you know, hangin' in there. You want a beer, son?" He responded as if he was oblivious to the fact that I was not comfortable with the situation.

I asked, "What's going on? You drinking now?" as my dad handed me a beer.

"Ahhh, just a couple here and there. No big deal," he said, shrugging his shoulders, eyes still focused on the game.

"Okay. You sure about that?"

"Yeah, son. Ya know, we couldn't take SweetPea with us when we went to Hawaii because it cost too much feria. When she died while we were out there, I just couldn't handle it anymore. We went through hell in Hawaii, kid. Fuuucckiinn misery—your mom's family is insane. I will never talk to that Lena again. She tried to kill your mother!"

Lena, my mother's sister, and my mom always had a rocky relationship. After their parents died, something snapped in all of them. For Lena, this took the form of mental illness and thriving on drama, while for my mom, it meant numbing her pain with pharmaceuticals. My dad proceeded to explain that my aunt is completely unhinged. She put chemicals in my mom's shampoo to make her hair fall out and even went as far as putting poison in her food when they were staying with her. To this day, my mom swears it was out of jealousy, but I imagine there's more to the story.

So there he was, forced to close his store, dealing with my mom's addiction to pills, her crazy family, and his dog (his best friend) dying without him there. All this pain piled on to a lifetime of agony.

Still, I couldn't believe that he was making matters worse by drinking. He had proven in the past that he couldn't control his drinking, but somehow, he was blind to it. I, like him, was still living in the fantasy that I could control mine.

[ENCINITAS, CA —DECEMBER 2006]

It was less than a year since my dad had tried to commit suicide. My parents lost their apartment in the senior living community. They were so behind on rent that they were evicted and were living in their car. I drove through Encinitas, pulling behind the Vons parking lot where I spotted my parents' beaten two-door 1990 Hyundai Accent parked on the side of the road. The marine layer made the sky overcast, gray, and stale the way everything often felt on the California coast.

All of this was hard to wrap my head around, and I found myself fighting a lump in my throat, holding back tears as I approached the car.

"Hi, Mom and Dad."

"Hi, son," my dad said.

Mom followed with a sweet but ashamed, "Hi, Michael."

"How are you guys doing?" I asked, knowing exactly how they were doing.

"Eh, we're hanging in there," my dad said. "My back is killing me though. It's hard to sleep in the car."

Forever the victim, God bless her, my mom's eyes welled

up with tears. She fought them back best she could as she said, "I don't know how we ended up like this. I don't understand. We're good people. We don't deserve this." She sounded lost, like a child who genuinely had no idea how their actions could lead to this outcome.

Seeing them in such a state of weakness was hard to reconcile, but then again it was hard to come to terms with the fact that my parents were even still together. They had both gone their separate ways multiple times, my dad spending most of his time alone, occasionally seeking out prostitutes, while my mom moved us from place to place looking for a partner to take care of her. During one of the many moves, my mom met this guy Jerry, a stoner pill popper. They were on again and off again the same way she was with my dad. At one point she ended up marrying him and briefly moved us to Hawaii to be with him. I'll never forget when my dad learned about his existence. It was 1996, and we had just gone to this Mexican restaurant for dinner. When we got back to my dad's mattress shop, there was a voicemail on the answering machine.

My dad pressed play and it was a message from Jerry. He was drunk and slurring on the voicemail saying he wanted to talk to Alexandra, that he loved her and he was going to see her soon. My mom stood next to my dad just listening, not sure what to do or say. At that moment my dad snapped. He grabbed my mom by the head and pushed her head into the ground. She bit her tongue so hard that she almost bit it clear off. She was screaming, I was screaming, and my dad was flipping out telling her to get the fuck out of there, calling her a whore. I remember her open mouth filling with blood as we saw the split tongue.

Seeing the pain my parents caused each other was something I never got used to, but somehow, at the same time, it was all I knew, and I had grown to expect it. Still, seeing them so desperate, living in their car, the lump in my throat continued to grow.

"I wish I could help you guys. I'm not in a position to right now. I have roommates," I said, fighting off deep feelings of guilt, lost in thought, trying to find a solution but unable to. "Hopefully things will get better soon. I'm working really hard; I've taken multiple jobs to try to stay afloat. I wish I was in a place to help you guys, but I just can't right now. I'm sorry."

I hugged my mom tightly, "I'll call you later, okay?"

Quickly, I turned to walk away, clenching my jaw as I gritted my teeth, my eyes filling with tears but refusing to let them fall. There were so many times that I wanted to tell them that I loved them but didn't know how. And to be honest, my mom said it as often as possible, but my dad couldn't say it. How can you give out love if you don't love yourself, or know what love really is? It's hard, and it just feels staged when you try to do it. Seeing them like that always made me feel guilty that I was pursuing my dream of surfing the world and getting paid to do it. It made me feel especially guilty to know that I was continually going on deep benders. I'd often feel that I should be doing everything I can to house and take care of them, but how do you help someone who doesn't want help? They didn't want to get sober, and neither did I.

We were lost.

The entire next year of my life was a blur. My drinking got completely out of hand. I did everything in my power to try and escape reality.

I would go on benders that would last anywhere from days up to months at a time. Drinking anything from cheap beer to vodka and malt liquor—anything I could get my hands on. I learned that if you bought an Old English or King Cobra 40-ounce it wasn't half bad as long as you poured yourself a glass of it, while keeping the bottle in the fridge, ice cold. It was when it started getting warm that it was hard to get down. When it was available, I was doing key flicks of coke, usually in the bathroom of dive bars, and boy was that a treat. At this point, I had absolutely no money, but people knew who I was in my small bubble from surfing, which meant free drinks were always coming my way. I know now that I was acting out the deep guilt and fear of my parents' homelessness and my surfing career collapsing. I would drink to leave all of it behind, drinking nonstop to stay in the fantasy of being better than, and less than, everyone at the same time.

[CARDIFF, CA —FEBRUARY 2007]

Already lit, I stumbled into The Gym, our local dive bar. This place was a shithole that always smelled like booze and vomit. Perfect for when you're belligerent. I dragged my roommate Steven out with me, and even though I was near blackout, I went hard, downing pints of red beer (V8 and beer). Tasty little bastards.

Not surprising at all, but Brad was there. Dude was always there. At the time, he was about fifty with blonde hair that, had he not been a surfer, would probably be gray by now. He had a potbelly but was still a bit of a lord.

"I'm telling you, you've got the talent, man," Brad said, well aware of the fact that he was clearly smoking my pole. "You're the next best thing to come out of this area. I've lived in this area my whole life, and you've got what it takes."

He was as delusional as I was.

"Thank you, I feel that. I really want it, man."

"And listen—don't take shit from anybody. You run this town. I've got your back," he said as he staggered around, beer in hand.

I shot the shit with Brad for a while, slurring my way through, one eye closed, trying to focus. Eventually, Steven and I made our way over to play some pool. At this point, I was so drunk, and I'd had my ego so stroked, that it was inevitable that things were going to go sour.

I saw this girl who worked at a local surf shop near my dad's store. She was fairly tall and thin. Curly blonde hair and beautiful sharp features. I'd had a crush on her since I was sixteen. I didn't even know her, but I had almost summoned up the courage to ask her to my senior prom. I had ended up getting set up with another girl for prom, so I didn't have to, thank God. I was hopeless with girls, and I did my best to keep them as far away from me as possible because of my home life. I was so embarrassed by my family, our home—or lack thereof—that it was easier to keep people at a distance, especially girls.

Now that I was drinking, I didn't give a shit. Alcohol takes all of your fears away. Alcohol made me invincible, and I had my own place to bring them back to. My friends called my room "the spider trap door." This is because, on more than one occasion, I'd wake up hungover and in a daze from the night before. It would be around 10:00 p.m., and my roommates, unbeknownst to me, would be having a party at our house. I would walk out of my door, see a girl I wanted, grab her, and invite her back into my room, all in the course of minutes. This is how much of a disgrace I had become. At the time I felt cool. This is what all of my heroes did, and society did its part to normalize and even encourage that behavior, or at least that's what I thought.

Here I was becoming my dad, a womanizer, and I didn't

even know it. Just like my dad had become a monster like his mom. She, too, turned to alcohol and couldn't—or wouldn't—take care of her kids. In 1962, when my dad was nine years old, he saw his mother, Bonnie, for the last time. All he can remember about how she looked is the constellation of freckles across her otherwise fair skin. Over time, he watched her complexion permanently redden due to alcoholism, coming close to matching her naturally red hair.

My dad heard the judge say, "What do you want to do with your two boys, Mrs. Millin?"

Followed by the cold, simple, response, "I don't want them."

The trauma continued to compound. Growing up without a father was one thing, but add a cold, alcoholic mother who couldn't take care of herself, let alone her kids. His life had become one form of neglect after another by the time he and his brother were moved to a home for boys that was more like a juvenile hall than a home for children. From there, the abuse only escalated. The two brothers would remain there, unwanted and unloved, until the age of eighteen. It's long been speculated that during this time they both were victims of molestation. We never talked about it in detail, but the signs were there. I never met my uncle; he was beaten to death in jail at the age of twenty, just a year younger than I was. I related to what my dad and my uncle went through. My dad didn't leave me to grow up in a children's home, but through his destructive behavior, he abandoned himself, ultimately abandoning me in the process.

"That chick is firing," I said to Steven.

"I know. Why don't you get in there?"

I walked over to her. I was always pretty good at acting sober, even when I had been drinking for days. Despite my mostly sober appearance, I was blocked by a group of her guy friends. Confused and angry, I made my way back over to Steven.

"These fucking kooks are blocking me."

"Fuck these guys."

We continued to shoot pool and drink red beers, finding ourselves still at the bar by the time they did last call and began kicking everyone out for closing time. As the bar closed, everyone stood around in the parking lot instead of immediately heading out.

I approached the girl again, only to have her group of guys block me yet again. I was so far gone by this point, just a bad combination of ego, alcohol, and belligerence.

"Hey, why don't you fuckin' kooks go back to Escondido," I slurred.

The group quickly had me circled. One of the guys completely blindsided me with a fist to the side of the face. I would have put up a bit of a fight if I had known I was in one. I dropped to the ground, and they started kicking me. Brad and Steven did what they could to help and got jumped as well. Steven really shouldn't be risking it to protect me (he was already semidisabled after he ended up in a coma from the last time he was jumped).

Brad yelled, "Hey, you motherfuckers, get off him!!"

Everyone was screaming—the people in the brawl but also the bystanders who were wondering what the hell was going on. The group proceeded to total Brad's new BMW that was parked nearby, kicking out the windows and denting the doors.

As soon as the focus was off of us, like cowards, we did our best drunk version of a military crawl out of there.

We got out of there as quickly as possible, letting Brad fend for himself. The moment we were clear from the brawl, we started running.

"Holy shit, dude." Steven gasped.

Holding my face, "Fuck, Steven, are you alright?"

"Yeah, dude, I'm okay. Are you?"

"I'm alright. Fuck those dickheads!!!" I said, high on adrenaline. "Come on, let's get home."

Once we were at a safe distance, we started walking. It was going to be a long walk home, so we took the quickest route possible, which meant walking along the train tracks, hobbling to the side when the train came through, then making the rest of our way on the Pacific Coast Highway. We made it across San Elijo Lagoon and into a nice neighborhood near Seaside—quiet, well-maintained, middle- to upper-class beach homes. Definitely not the version of Solana Beach I grew up in.

At 3:00 a.m., drunk, beaten, and completely exhausted, I wanted nothing more than to stop walking. "Steven, let's go to Jason's house. They're out of town, and I know where they hide the keys to the Chevy."

"Yeah, man, sure, let's go," Steven said.

We saw the 1963 Chevy parked in front of the house. I grabbed the keys from the hiding place and jumped in the truck. I was trying to get it started. It was an old, loud, three-on-the-tree transmission. I kept trying; I was desperate to get home.

"It won't start. Damn it, it won't start!"

"Keep trying. Dude, I'm fucking exhausted," Steven said, as if his face hadn't already told me that. Out of nowhere, the neighbor showed up in his night robe.

"Hey, what are you guys doing?" he asked politely but also clearly suspicious and rightfully so.

Startled, I said, "Oh hey...umm...we were in the area, and my friend was interested in buying Jason's truck, so we thought we'd see if it would at least start. Sorry, did we wake you?"

Like no shit, we woke him.

"You really think that's a good idea right now? It's three o'clock in the morning," he said.

"Umm, probably not. We'll get outta here. So sorry about that..." I trailed off, hopping out of the truck and putting the keys back before stumbling off into the darkness with Steven.

[BYRON BAY, AUSTRALIA —APRIL 2007]

At the time, I was riding for a company called Zoo York. I had just accepted an offer to join their pro team. Being on their team meant that I received endless amounts of clothing, all-expenses-paid trips, a small salary, and a photo incentive, meaning that every time I got a photo in a magazine with their logo showing, I got paid. On this one occasion, they set me up on an all-expenses-paid trip to Australia. They teed everything up for me. All I had to do was reach out to locally based surf photographers and land some photos to get exposure for the brand. The photos were set to pair with a feature that I was going to be writing for a San Diego–based magazine. It was all laid out for me. I couldn't have asked for a better opportunity.

The first week of the trip was an absolute blowout. I partied nonstop from the moment I landed in Australia. I went out every night chasing after girls, living the "dream." To be completely honest, once I started drinking, a big part of my dream was to go to these countries, these places I had always imagined going to, and partying as hard as I possibly could. I always had this feeling like, I could go to these other countries and find the peace and excitement that I was looking for through partying, whether it was Australia or Bali or anywhere in the world. I really just wanted to go there to party, to experience the culture, the women, and the drinking and everything that goes with it—and I never found what I was looking for. I thought that somehow this would fulfill me if I could go to these places and experience these things, but it never did. It always left me feeling empty and unsatisfied.

A week into the trip, there I was at one of the most incredible breaks in the world, the SuperBank on the Gold Coast in Australia. I was paddling out at the endless right point break, and out of nowhere it felt like I had a pinched nerve in my shoulder. I immediately felt a sense of dread—this feeling that when good things are on the horizon, something inevitably comes in to take that away. I was there to get work done and I knew that this shoulder would be an issue. Not to mention, I had fucked around for the entire week prior to this, so I had zero content on hand.

Instead of resting and doing what I could to get a single shot, I continued partying with my crew.

Later that week, I was with Mark and we were about to have a big night. We were already pretty faded and had been drinking for a few hours. By the time evening rolled around, we were able to get some ecstasy through one of his contacts, and so it was on. We were going down to the Byron Bay Beach Club. We don't have clubs like this in the States. The place was across the street from the beach, half indoor, half outdoor with this casual beach-turned-rave atmosphere. It was so unique, not like one of those New York City or Miami types of places. They had electronic music long before it was mainstream in the States and was all around a good time. Aussies really know how to party.

We went hard all night, and most of it turned into a blackout at some point. Like most nights, I either lost or ditched my crew. Part of me always liked losing the crew I was with. Even when I was drinking on benders, I've always liked to go and do my own thing. There's something about being independent that I've always liked.

So I lost them.

I ended up linking up with this random group of Australians I had never met before. The guy seemed cool, and I think he was. I honestly don't even remember what he looked like, but I remember this sort of mist-like character along with maybe four or so other people. Come to think of it, they might not even have been real people. I could've just made all of this up, but anyway, we went hard together, and then he was sort of just like, "Hey, mate, have you ever tried acid?"

I said, "Uh, no," but when I was faded, especially on ecstasy, I was about willing to do anything. I was in this place where I just figured, *All right, I've already gone further than I ever thought I would with trying drugs and alcohol; I might as well try everything now that I'm here.*

As the sun was starting to rise, I found myself at this guy's house as we put acid tabs on our tongues. This, for me, after days and days of drinking. An absolute bender, and I was exhausted, basically coming down from alcohol, and I was just wondering, *What's going on here? What's going to happen?* For a long time, it seemed as though nothing was happening, but after an hour it started to kick in. Immediately I thought to myself, *Wow, I need to get home! I gotta get back to the house, and I don't even know where I am.* I don't remember if I did a Batman and just bailed without saying goodbye to that crew. I might have. I also might have said "Hey, I gotta get out of here," but who knows? Either way, I stumbled out of there.

I knew that we were somewhere near the beach, and if I could just make my way there, all I had to do was start walking south. I walked from Byron Bay to Lennox Head on the beach, peaking on acid. I later came to find out it is a good eleven-mile walk. It was a blur of a walk, but I somehow ended up making it back.

Mark just looked at me as I walked in the door. "Fuck, what happened to you?" he said, laughing and shaking his head as he took in my current state. "Man, we figured you'd make it back somehow," he said, still cracking up as I told him about all of my shenanigans.

Our host suggested we go for a swim at the pond. It's an all-natural tea tree oil pond, unlike anything I had ever seen before. These ponds are sacred and were a place where aborigines used to give birth. It was incredibly clean, refreshing, and healing. I remember going down there with the guys, jumping into the pond, and opening my eyes in the water. The tea tree makes the water this clear red. And so, here I was, underwater, moving around in the clear red, peaking on acid. It honestly felt like I was on Mars. I felt like Arnie in *Total Recall*, the original. I was so mesmerized that the guys even got to the point where they were like, "Fuck, I wish I was on some acid."

I don't know if I got anything out of it other than frying my brain, but it was wild.

~ ~ ~

Days bled into night and we found ourselves on a nonstop bender throughout my entire time in Australia. We were tying on another night at the Beach Club in Byron Bay. Mark and I, along with the rest of our crew, were going hard, you know, drinking as much as possible, just pure debauchery, laughing our asses off, meeting random Australians, chasing girls, and again, I lost the guys.

It was late so I sat at the bar. This bartender clocked me, walked up, and asked me what I'd like. She noticed my accent. Australian girls, like most girls, love an accent, and they are worse than most dudes when it comes to being down for casual sex (or "a root," as they call it). So, I told her I was from the States, and she looked me in the eyes and said, "You're on ecstasy, aren't you?" It's really not that hard to tell. When you're on ecstasy, your pupils get massive; it's almost like a deer in headlights.

I said, "Yes," and she said, "I want you to stay here, on this barstool, until I get off my shift. I'm gonna take care of you."

I said, "Okay," and just sat there, blown away.

I stayed put throughout the rest of the night, thinking how much she looked like a porcelain doll. She had dark curly hair that sat just above the collarbone and this pale skin. She gave me drink after drink. I didn't even have to pay for them.

When she got off her shift, she came and grabbed me by my hand and walked me to her car. I went with her to her house, and we proceeded to have sex, only I was so drunk and numb on drugs that I couldn't even really get an erection.

I mean I sort of got it in there for a while, I remember, but I was just so fucked that I couldn't even really perform. She was a good sport about it. She was super kind, gave me water, and asked if there was anything she could do. I said, "No," and started to get dressed to head out. Before I left, she said to make sure I saw her before I flew home. I couldn't believe it, but for me, the attitude around sex that Aussies had was perfect for where I was at. Fake intimacy, one and done, without any fear of rejection.

By that point, it was already sunrise. I was still completely wrecked and ended up hitchhiking back to where I was staying.

[SOLANA BEACH, CA —MAY 2007]

I landed back in California in an absolute daze, with no money, no car, and shoulder was destroyed. To top it off, I had no health insurance, and I was drinking every day. My body and my brain felt totaled.

What did I expect? I had spent an entire month on an insane bender with my buddies, got absolutely zero work done, and quite possibly fucked up my brain in the process. For a while, I was worried I had done permanent damage. I even had some close friends mention to me, "Hey Mikey, man, I don't know what happened to you in Australia, but you don't seem quite the same, ya know?" That really scared me.

Here I was, flat broke, back in Solana Beach. I couldn't go to my parents for help since they were homeless.

I met up with my good friend Morgan. He was always there when I needed a sounding board. He is a big guy, six foot one with blue eyes, blonde curly hair with a surfer's golden tan on what would otherwise be fair skin. He looks just like an adult-sized version of the Gerber baby, which is exactly what everyone calls him.

Morgan couldn't solve everything for me, but he did have a suggestion about my messed-up shoulder. "I know this chiropractor, Dr. Idris; he works with tons of athletes from the NFL to surfers. He's a really cool guy, and I think he would see you. I'll reach out to him and introduce you."

I went and saw Dr. Idris as soon as possible. I walked him through my situation and let him know that I didn't have any health insurance and that I really couldn't afford this. Immediately, he jumped in. "Let me get you an MRI. Don't worry about the cost; we can do this pro bono." MRIs aren't cheap, so I was beyond grateful.

The MRI results came back, and it completely freaked me out. It showed a nickel-sized tumor nestled within the bone of my left humerus. As great as he was, Dr. Idris didn't have the best poker face. He looked me in the eyes and said, "Hey, I have no idea what this is. It could be malignant cancer—we don't know, but we've got to get you in the hands of a specialist as soon as possible."

He was incredible, an absolute godsend. He set everything up for me, helping me get in touch with people who could get me health insurance. It was called CMS, County Medical Services, for people who were low-income, in poverty—people like me who didn't have coverage. The process took a long time, at least a month or two of jumping through hoops to get approval.

Anyone who cares about, or even remotely respects, themself would have seen this as a wake-up call. They would have done what they could to get healthy and to optimize their body to heal faster. Not me. I was so angry at my body, and I felt like such a victim that I couldn't even see how my actions were affecting me physically. Not only that—I just didn't even care anymore.

While I was dealing with my shoulder and drinking to oblivion, my cousin Mark continued learning what not to do. He got invited on a massive surfing trip to Iceland with some of the top pros from our area and ended up getting a double-page spread in *Surfer Magazine*. I kept thinking that I could have been there in Iceland if I wasn't unhealthy. Like polar opposites, I was going lower and lower and my cousin's career was peaking, expanding, and hitting a whole new level. It sent me even deeper into the bottle. I disappeared into drugs and alcohol as my shoulder got worse and worse every day. I was in agony.

Come to find out, after getting health insurance and working with a specialist who did some tests on my arm, they found out that it was actually a benign tumor called a chondroblastoma. They didn't know what caused it, but it was causing a lot of pain and pressure in my humerus.

Chondroblastomas are actually pretty rare. It's basically a buildup of cartilage cells that form a tumor. While the doctor didn't know the cause, I got the feeling that I had been treating myself so badly, for so long, with self-destruction through drugs and alcohol that this popped up in my system as a warning or system-wide alert that I was shutting down.

I shut down all right. I turned this into a year of absolute destruction because even after I got the surgery there was another eight months of healing before I could surf again. During that time, I went deeper into a dark bender. Completely lost myself.

~ ~ ~

When my shoulder finally healed, I emerged from the cave I had created for myself. I started surfing again and laying off the booze. I even started getting back on some surf trips. Zoo York arranged for a trip to Newfoundland on the east coast of Canada. It was one of the most special trips I have ever been on in terms of wave discovery. There was a purity to it. No one around, incredibly cold, and raw beauty everywhere you looked. Raw beauty and wild blueberries growing along the coast.

For a kid from San Diego, this was really special. We'd be walking back, boards under our arms, shivering, picking and eating fresh blueberries off the bushes.

The locals up there were the closest thing to present-day pirates that I have ever seen. They have this accent that I really couldn't understand. They were speaking English but it sounded like, "Ay matey blimey landlubber hornswoggle reclaimed hearties briny deep lad." It was like something from another world, but they were so genuine, raw, and weathered by the sea.

As great as it was to be there, I had a really hard time on the trip because I wasn't where I wanted to be either mentally or physically. I was out of shape after just having gone through a year or two of complete self-destruction, and the waves were really critical and dangerous. I hate to say it, but I didn't have it in me.

One of the guys on the trip kept saying, "Man, you need to step it up," and trust me, I really wanted to. The first few days I was putting myself on the line, risking myself in some super heavy waves that broke on a shallow reef shelf. Ultimately, I started to back off in the coming days to keep from getting injured. Mark came to my defense, letting the guy know I just came out of shoulder surgery and to give me a break. We've had our rocky moments, but my cousin had my back.

[ENCINITAS, CA —MARCH 2008]

I was chatting with my surf team manager, Fred. Fred was a stiff guy, but he loved me and wanted what was best for me, and I knew that. He was beyond blunt and sarcastic. About six feet tall with a bowl cut and a bald spot that had formed a skin yarmulke.

"So what's been going on?" Fred asked. "You been surfing?"

"Ahhh, not really. A little bit."

Fred, half joking, said, "Well, whatta we paying you for?" Completely casual and matter-of-fact, Fred followed it up with, "Mike, you're an alcoholic." He said it with a slight grin, but he was serious. "Maybe you should try AA. There's a place down there on Second Street."

Fred had said this to me once before, more in passing than a serious conversation, but this time...this time, he really meant it.

My blood was boiling. I was gritting my teeth at the mention of AA. Alcoholics Anonymous was where all the losers ended up. The homeless people, or the ones who were too weak to control the amount of drugs or alcohol they consumed. At least that's what I thought. Later I would come to find out that some of the most humble, creative, successful people on the planet are sitting in the rooms of Alcoholics Anonymous, with long-term sobriety. Over the years, I have sat next to some of my heroes, in meetings of AA. People that I thought I would never in a million years meet. Alcoholics Anonymous is like a hidden world.

I said nothing. I just clenched my jaw and kept my mouth shut. I hated hearing people tell me this. I couldn't bear the idea that I was different from anyone else, let alone that I had a problem I couldn't control. I would immediately get embarrassed, and that feeling completely took over. I changed the subject as quickly as I could.

"I'll start getting some work done. That shoulder surgery really set me back. I'm working on getting in shape. Thank you for believing in me." I was thanking him for believing in me, but I didn't believe in myself. Not anymore at least.

I was completely out of control. My life was falling apart, and instead of accepting the help that multiple people were offering, I chose self-destruction every chance I got. I had perfected self-sabotage. I would drink all night, knowing that the next morning was an important photo shoot. I would wake up still drunk and go straight to cracking open beers, completely blowing everything off, not once thinking about calling to let them know I wasn't coming. To make matters worse, I was continuing to teach Mark what not to do. He got super focused, showing up to all of the shoots and opportunities for sponsorship, ultimately, getting exposure in all of the mainstream surf magazines.

Spiraling out of control mentally and physically, I dropped

by Morgan's house. I needed to be around someone kind, someone to help ground me. Morgan really was a gentle giant. We used to tease him that he was tickling his succulents and would joke around saying shit like "Squash flavor? Oh, my favorite baby food."

When I got to Morgan's, I just sort of sat there quietly. I felt defeated and didn't have much to say. "What's been going on, dude? I haven't seen ya around," Morgan said, looking up from his newest addition to the already obsessive succulent collection.

"I don't know, man. I've been drinking too much. I feel like shit. I don't know what to do," I said, probably looking just as lost as I felt.

Without missing a beat, Morgan replied, "Mikey, you're an alcoholic, dude." His voice was compassionate, but he said it so quickly, so bluntly, that I couldn't handle it.

I began to turn away, positioning myself to leave. "Fuck, dude. I'm fine. Why don't you worry about yourself," I fired back at him. This was my default response.

I was so fractured hearing him say that, so massively in denial, that I just couldn't be there anymore.

"Mikey, wait. I'm just worried about ya. I care about ya, man."

I could tell that Morgan felt for me, that he was genuinely sorry for setting me off, but more so that he was sorry I was like this. His sincerity only made me feel worse and more ashamed.

My body tensed up. "Yeah, whatever. I'm sorry but I just gotta go right now. I'll hit you later," I said as I left the property.

By the time I got home, I had replayed the conversation

with Morgan in my mind a million times. I couldn't shake it. The words *you're an alcoholic* taunting me. That afternoon I curled up in my bed, tucked tightly into a ball, and sank into the comfort of a deep depression.

There was a part of me that loved these deep depressions. I could go into days of exiting the Matrix. If I was in bed for two to three days, I could completely unplug from reality and plug into whatever show was popular at the time, watching five seasons straight. Sometimes I would just lie there nude, jerking off. More to my imagination than to porn. I never was a big porn guy. I'd go through phases every once in a while, but I was never really that into it, and honestly it wasn't what I was looking for when I closed the shades and crawled under my blankets. This depressed time meant that I wouldn't have to really live or face the life that I had created. I'd get up to take a piss and that's it. I'd have food and a gallon of water next to my bed and just disappear for days.

[ENCINITAS, CA —JUNE 2008]

Sometime this year, Mark and I rented an apartment with a buddy of ours. It was one of those low-income apartment complexes in a Latino neighborhood. The apartment building was pretty much filled with Mexicans who were working in landscaping, restaurants in town, or the horse race stables down the road. They often had ten to fifteen people, maybe more, in each room to make ends meet.

Our place was perfect for us. Mark and his girlfriend at the time took the master bedroom, our buddy grabbed the guest room, and I took the loft. It had this cheap metal staircase going up to it and this strange hidden room through the closet door. Imagine a full-size room hidden behind the back closet wall, the entrance being a waist-high hole that you had to duck down to enter.

I was so excited to have this place, but at the same time, my parents were still homeless and that really ate at me. I drove down behind the Vons parking lot where they kept their Hyundai parked off to the side. Every time I saw their car there it felt like a hand reaching in and squeezing my heart.

"Mom, I can't handle seeing you living this way."

"I know, Michael," she said quietly, humiliated that her son had to keep seeing her like this. "We're hoping we get government assistance soon. If we get it, we can get a home," she said, looking down as if she couldn't bear to look me in the eyes. It was obvious that she was hanging on to hope by a thread.

"It's been rough," my dad added. "We have a hard time finding a place to park at night, and the heat is always on our back. Plus, it's hard for the two of us to sleep in here."

My heart couldn't take anymore. The idea of my mom struggling to sleep in that piece of shit car while cops were always making them move was unbearable. Add my dad's moods and drinking to the mix, and their situation was the epitome of a living hell. I had to do something.

"I have an extra room," I said, already knowing this was crazy, but it was the only option. "It's nothing special, but let me put Mom up for a little while. My roommate's not gonna like it, but we just have to do what we have to do right now."

"Thank you, son," my dad said, accepting the offer on behalf of my mom.

That night I helped my mom set up in the hidden closet.

[ENCINITAS, CA —JUNE 2008]

I came home late with a girl one night. Not just any girl. This was Anna, the girl I had had a crush on for years. I had many crushes, but Anna was definitely near the top of that list. She was five foot ten with dark wavy hair and an olive complexion. Absolutely beautiful. She rode a longboard and was a graceful surfer. I couldn't believe she wanted to come home with me. I never thought I would have a chance with her.

I was too embarrassed, and honestly, far more interested in being with her to tell her that my mom was living in the closet. I knew she was posted up in there, but I was so drunk that I hoped I could get laid and pull it off without Anna or my mom knowing.

The sex was passionate but we were both drunk. It wasn't what I thought it would be. It's strange how it's like that a lot of the time. I didn't feel the connection with her that I had expected to. We passed out immediately afterward.

In the middle of the night, Anna heard a sound that woke her. I heard it too, but didn't dare move. My mom crawled out of the hole in the closet. Anna just lay there watching her creep out into the darkness like a horror movie while I was pretending to be sleeping. I felt my entire body tense up as Anna silently freaked out. There was absolutely no way I was going to let either of them know I was awake. I was too mortified and too drunk to deal with it. I let myself drift back to sleep knowing full well I was going to have to acknowledge it in the morning. But still somehow wishing I wouldn't have to.

When the morning came, I pretended to be asleep as long as possible. The moment I rolled over, Anna immediately shot up in bed.

"Holy shit, someone came out of your closet last night!!"

"Oh yeah, sorry about that," I said, humiliated but playing it off like everything was okay. "There's another room, a secret room that's a full-size bedroom, through the closet. I know it's kind of weird, but my mom is staying here right now."

Anna was so visibly freaked out. She was quickly getting dressed while laughing (clearly out of awkwardness and discomfort).

"Oh my God! She came out of the hole in the closet in the middle of the night; it almost gave me a heart attack!!"

Laughing it off, I said, "Holy shit!" I froze up and was speechless.

"I need to get to work; can you give me a ride?" she said, laughing it off, and clearly still in shock, but also trying to make light of the situation.

The next day, I was thinking of what it must have been like for my mom to stand there, waiting at the closet entrance for her son to finish because she had to pee. Yeah, let's just say that this is a memory I'll never forget, and trust me, I drank enough to try.

After a full day of doing an odd job, which consisted of manual labor, I came home numb, looking to pass out. My mom came out of the small opening to the secret room. Immediately I felt a rush of embarrassment come over me; it was like a massive wave to the head. My face began to turn red. Looking back now, I realize that it wasn't just embarrassment; it was also anger. I was so angry that my mom couldn't take care of herself, that she had gotten to a point where she had nowhere else to go but my shitty little home, which I could barely afford to keep afloat.

"Hi, son, how was your day?"

Awkward, hungover, and defeated, I responded, "It was fine, Mom."

"Oh, okay. So who was that girl last night?"

I cringed. "Oh, Mom. What the fuck? What happened? What did you see or hear?"

Possibly more embarrassed than I was, she said, "I don't know, were you getting some?"

"Mom. I can't right now, I'm...I need to sleep; I have work in the morning."

"Oh, okay, sorry, son," she said with the same look of disgust she gave my father, before sinking back into the closet.

Shaking my head in disbelief, I wound my way down the spiral staircase to the kitchen. I cracked open a beer, downing it as quickly as I could to erase this moment from my mind. After a couple of cold ones, I made my way back up the stairs and completely passed out.

[ENCINITAS, CA —JULY 2008]

Not long after the now infamous closet incident, I was having a few drinks with my mom, Mark, and our neighbor Katie. To be honest, we really didn't know her that well, but she was always friendly, so we invited her over. It was always nice to have someone new to drink with.

"So, whatta you been up to?" I asked her.

"Ahhh, you know, just working mostly," Katie responded.

At this point, my dad, Nicholas, showed up. Unannounced, uninvited, and drunk. In his usual fashion he was loud, obnoxious, rude, a disgrace.

"Damn, you fine girl," my dad said.

Incredibly uncomfortable and not sure what to say, Katie responded, "Ahhh, thanks."

"Dad?? Chill out," I jumped in, mortified.

"What, kid? I'm just sayin', she's fine. I wouldn't mind a piece of that."

Everyone in the room went silent while simultaneously looking at my mom to see her reaction. My mom was too pilled out to really process it. We just sat there in the most awkward silence, observing this drunk old man. For me, this was a defining moment, a painful godsend in a way.

I saw my dad for exactly who he was. I saw his massive ego, the unbelievable level of self-pride, selfishness, and distortion of reality. Seeing my dad in this light felt like looking into a mirror for the first time. Finally, I saw my own behavior, and I understood why everyone had been telling me that I had a drinking problem. I knew how similar I was to my dad, and I saw what I had become by observing the man right in front of me. In this moment, in my heart, I knew I needed to quit drinking but didn't know how.

"On that note, I gotta go," I said, trying to put an end to the awkwardness. "Mom and Dad, let's get going."

Completely ignoring me and unsurprisingly still wanting to talk about himself, my dad said, "Kid, did I ever tell you about your Uncle Barry?"

I didn't respond. Mark, Katie, and I continued to sit in awkward silence as my dad proceeded to set the scene.

"You know, back in 1987, me and your Uncle Barry had this stand to sell furniture on the side of the road. One night, we were completely messed up. Barry was high on heroin, but that motherfucker wanted the keys to our truck. When I said no, he came after me with a gun, and I threw a chair at his face."

Mark tried to cut him off. "Come on, Uncle Nick, we don't need to talk about this."

"I got him good, split his face wide open, blood everywhere. That crazy bastard deserved it after unloading three rounds at my head. If I hadn't unloaded the gun earlier that day, I would be dead."

We all sat there in shock as my dad continued.

"Fuck, kid. He was bleeding like crazy. I gave him a towel to wrap up his face so I could take him to the hospital. The whole way there, Barry just went on and on saying, 'I'm gonna fucking kill you. They aren't gonna find your bones. You're dead.' I wasn't going to wait around to find out if he meant it. I stopped in front of the hospital. The moment he closed the car door, I took off."

I'll say this about Uncle Barry: dude had the look of a stone-cold killer. He had this quiet intensity and a completely dead look in his eyes. Let's just say that it was a good thing that Uncle Barry lived in Wyoming and could hunt wild game freely.

My mom surprised us by joining in. "Is that when you drove straight from LA to Wyoming to see me at my sister's?"

"Yeah, I'll never forget it. I was so drunk by that point that I needed a driver, so I picked up this hitchhiker somewhere just outside of LA. It was great; I let him drive as I cracked open a couple of beers and shot the shit with him. I think I even offered him a job or something."

"That's right, Michael, your dad picked up a hitchhiker and tried to bring him into your Auntie Joanna's place. She was not having it; you know how strong she is. She told your dad to pack up and head back home."

My mom was right. Auntie Joanna is strong. She looks like an older version of my mom, but that's where the similarities end. Auntie Joanna looks exactly like you'd imagine for a Native American woman living on a reservation—she is practical, dresses humbly, and holds a lifetime of wisdom in her eyes. She lost the childlike innocence that my mom still has. You could say that she has experienced and seen too much to continue walking through life being naive.

"So, Dad, what did you do? Did you let Auntie Joanna kick you out?" I asked, hoping he would wrap the story, but also sort of curious at this point.

"Yeah, Mikey, I wasn't looking for more drama. I drove the whole way back to LA solo. The guy I picked up couldn't handle it, so I just went on my own. It was fucking crazy; I still can't believe that fucker tried to kill me."

My dad finally wrapped the story. Yet again, the entire room was silent. Nobody knew how to respond to this. Katie was staring at my mom, clearly wondering why on earth she was back with my dad. The awkward tension continued to intensify until it was too much for me. I put my hand on my dad's shoulder and started to usher him toward the door.

"Alright, Pops, well, I really gotta get going now. I'm meeting up with some buddies, and I'm already late."

I finally got my dad out of the apartment. My mom looked defeated and took the opportunity to dismiss herself and hide out in the closet, further numbing herself on a mix of Ambien and methadone. I really felt for my mom as she had been so embarrassed by my dad that night, but for as long as I can remember she had been popping pills to avoid the reality of her life. I don't know when it started, but I do know that her uncle molested her when she was a teenager, shortly after her mom had died. Out of fear, and later out of shame, she said nothing—not to anyone. I am the first to say that yes, her life was hard, but she made it even harder on herself by choosing this lifestyle.

And what did I do? I decided that if I was going to get sober, I first needed to go as hard as possible, to really get this thing out of my system, and what better time to start than now?

[ENCINITAS, CA —JULY 2008]

To stop drinking was to enter hell.

I had been drinking and doing drugs for what felt like so long even though I was only twenty-three. I thought about the first time I ever did drugs—well, speed at least. I was eleven years old and my cousin, Kai, was living with us. By us, I mean my mom, my stepdad, Jerry, and me.

At the time, Kai was twenty-two. He grew up in Hawaii, and I looked up to him a lot. He was such a cool guy. He introduced me to a lot of music that I ended up loving as a kid, like Tool, Rob Zombie, and Nine Inch Nails, which is weird because surfers really didn't listen to that kind of music. Most of the guys I knew listened to Sublime, Blink 182, and Jack Johnson. I just didn't get it; that music felt too happy to me. I was always drawn to dark music as a kid.

When I was young, I knew that Kai was always into drugs, but he treated me like I was a friend, like an adult, and nobody had ever done that. I always used to think that was so cool back then but, looking at it now, it actually wasn't.

He was doing speed one night with his buddy at the house, and I said I wanted to try it—and he let me.

So there I was at eleven years old, having just snorted a line of speed. I wasn't sure what I was supposed to do. I just cleaned. I remember sweeping, vacuuming, mopping. I sort of just kept cleaning all night until I fell asleep.

Twenty years passed before I saw Kai again, and when I did, he apologized to me. I'll never forget it. He looked me dead in the eyes and said, "Man, I'm so sorry that I did that to you. To be honest with you, if someone did that to one of my kids, I would kill them. I'm really sorry."

I'm not sure if this had set me on my future path of drinking and using, but it certainly didn't help. The thing is that quitting drugs wasn't really an issue for me; my issue was drinking.

I would go into terror over the thought of stopping drinking. I knew I needed to do it, and I told myself I was going to—just not yet. You see, stopping drinking meant that I was going to need to start facing all my problems.

So, even if it was four o'clock in the morning, if I ran out of alcohol, I would make my way to the twenty-four-hour liquor store near my house. I would walk in, give the clerk a friendly hello, and walk over to grab an eighteen-pack of beer. Once I had the beer, I would make my way toward the front door and just punch through the door, making a run for it. I got away with it a couple of times with two different clerks before I met my match.

The last time I tried it, I walked in the front door, and this Samoan lady working the checkout recognized me. I knew she had clocked me but I still had to try. I booked it to grab the eighteen-pack as she went and blocked the door. When I'm determined, when I really put my mind to something, I put it in my mind that I'm going to achieve that goal at any cost. Even though this looked impossible, I was still going to give it my all. There we were, at the front of the liquor store, me versus the Samoan lady. I did my best to juke her out with a Barry Sanders move but man, she had me. She was shouting loudly to stop this.

I put down the pack of beer and shimmied past her. Once I put it down, she was good to let me go.

[ENCINITAS, CA —AUGUST 2008]

A few weeks after my dad dropped by and rambled on about Uncle Barry, I was watching TV with my mom. I was completely hungover, coming down from drugs, while my mom was on a self-medicating spree of her own. We heard a knock on the door. We were both in such a messed-up state of being that we were genuinely confused about the sound of someone knocking on the door, let alone having any idea who it could be.

I got up slowly and made my way to the door. I was moving like I was in my seventies, not my twenties.

"Hey, Dad," I said, thinking to myself, *What now?*

Sobbing, "I'm scared, son."

"What's up, Dad?" I said, somewhat dismissive.

"I'm really scared, son," he said, almost incoherent through the deep sobs and gasps for air.

Shifting from annoyed to concerned, "Tell me, Dad. I'm here."

My mom hurried to the door, terrified. "What's going on?"

"I swallowed this whole bottle of pills, son," he said,

defeated, as he put the bottle into the palm of my hand. "I mean it this time. I don't wanna live anymore."

A gripping pain and that familiar feeling of fear took hold in the pit of my stomach. "Oh Dad."

My mom, immediately panicking despite being completely strung out, said, "Oh shit, Poppa."

Staying calm to help keep my parents calm, "Come on, Dad, we have to get you to the hospital." Turning to my mom, I said, "Mom, hurry up and grab your things."

"I'm scared, son," my dad said as I threw one of his arms over my shoulder, letting him rest his weight on me as I carried him out of the apartment to my car. I urgently raced to the hospital, doing everything I could not to freak out.

"Oh, Poppa, why did you do this?!" my mom cried.

"Oh, Momma."

My mom would later tell me that she spent the drive to the hospital in absolute terror, reliving the moment she lost her parents. It was 1978; she was fifteen years old sitting in the waiting room of a Hawaii hospital with her family. Young Joanna walked into the room and simply said, "She's gone."

When her mom died, the whole world seemed to have stopped for my mom. Her life was never the same from that moment onward. Both of her parents were dead, her father passing six years earlier from a brain aneurysm.

My mom was pulled out of her trance by the sound of my voice as I said, "We're almost there, Dad, hang on. Everything's gonna be okay." I watched her wipe the tears away, assuming it was about my dad, now realizing she was crying over the loss of her innocence. She was crying over the life she found herself in as a result.

I was halfway out of the car by the time I reached the emergency room doors, throwing the car in park and sprinting in to speak to the clerk.

Hyped up on adrenaline, I explained, "I need help. My dad attempted to kill himself by swallowing a bottle of pills."

"Okay, where is he?" the nurse said calmly but concerned.

"He's in the car with my mom," I said, running back toward my car while ushering the nurse to come with me.

"Come on, Dad. They're gonna get you in," I said as I carried him toward the doors where a nurse was coming with a wheelchair. He was sobbing uncontrollably with tears and snot all over his face.

"Come on, Poppa," my mom chimed in.

The nurse wheeled my dad away, and I turned to hug my mom.

We nervously sat in the waiting room while the doctors pumped his stomach.

After some time, a doctor came our way. He was older, probably in his sixties, bald with small reading glasses. Looking down at the clipboard to make sure he was getting our names right, he greeted us, "Hello, Michael? Mrs. Millin?"

"Yes, sir," I said, shifting in my chair.

The doctor took a look at my mom and then back at me. I could tell he immediately recognized that she was on something, and he wasn't going to bother explaining things to her. "So it looks like your dad is going to make it. It's still hard to tell, at this point, what the fallout will be, but he is stable for now. We were able to pump most of the medication out of his stomach, but we're going to have to put him on a seventy-two-hour hold after the suicide attempt."

"Okay, sir, we understand. Thank you," I said, not sure what else there really was to say.

"You've got it. Try to take it easy tonight; you guys have been through a lot, and this is not easy," he said, as he handed us a pamphlet with support options.

I took the pamphlet and sat there staring at the tile floor. I was so scared, terrified. My parents were both checking out; my dad had now tried to kill himself multiple times, drilling me deeper and deeper into pain, feeling lost, crushed, and sad. Nothing in my life was stable. I didn't have enough rent money to pay for my place, the place that my mom was still living in the closet of, I didn't have consistent work, and there was nothing about my life that was stable or healthy.

[ENCINITAS, CA —AUGUST 2008]

Two weeks after my dad's latest suicide attempt, I hit the depths of despair. I was at an all-time low. It felt like I was drowning in my own pain, in the pain my father carried with him every day, and in the pain my mother kept at bay with pills. I was angry at myself for what my life had become but also so afraid of change—of the idea of trying and potentially failing.

Mark had just gotten home. My two buddies and I were hanging out, drinking and chopping lines of cocaine.

Mark snapped, "What the hell are you doing?"

"Yo," I said, completely ignoring the irritation in his voice as I proceeded to snort a line of coke.

"You fuckin' idiot. You're gonna die," Mark said, storming out of the room with fury.

I took another swig of my beer while my friends sat there quietly feeling awkward.

I didn't care.

By 4:00 a.m. we were finally bringing the night to a close. We hadn't even gone out. We just stayed in all night telling drug stories, drinking, and doing more lines of the devil's dandruff.

"Fuck, I have to wake up at 6:00 a.m. for work," I groaned.

"Yeah, man, I better get home," my buddy said.

"Hey, Steven, do you have any of the Seroquel?" I asked, still amped up on all the cocaine. "I'm not gonna be able to sleep."

Steven pulled out the pills, crushed them up, and cut three lines. We each snorted a line and called it a night.

When I finally woke up, it was 9:00 a.m. I was three hours late for work. I was numb; it was as if the Seroquel had completely negated the cocaine. I felt like somebody had tranquilized me, but they hadn't. I had done this to myself. I scrambled to get dressed, wanting so badly to be fast but unable to. I moved slowly as my body went into a cold sweat. I grabbed my skateboard and booked it out of the apartment the best I could and headed to work.

I showed up at the valet stand of the Hilton Hotel, haggard, pale, almost gray, completely covered in sweat.

"Hey, Jeff, I'm so sorry I'm late. My van broke down."

"Oh shit, alright dude. I was wondering what happened to you," Jeff said kindly, completely buying it.

"Yeah, it broke down. I got a ride and skated the rest of the way," I said, holding up the skateboard as proof.

"Okay, man, it's gonna start getting busy, so if you wanna take over, that'd be great."

"Yeah, absolutely. I'm on it. Sorry again."

Jeff was right; it did get busy. I was running back and forth parking cars. Rich people handing me the keys to their luxury cars while I was sweating and parched. All of a sudden this horrible pain came over me. It felt like my heart was coming out of my chest. I dropped to the ground, clenching my chest, terrified.

"Hey, you alright, Mikey?" one of the other valets asked while running over to me.

Winded, cold, still sweating, I managed a reply. "I don't know what's going on, but it feels like I'm having a heart attack."

"Oh, shit, dude. Should I get you some help? Let me grab Jeff."

The two of them ran over to me, clearly concerned. "You alright, Mikey?" Jeff asked.

"I'm not sure what's going on," I said, out of breath. "My heart's in a lot of pain. I was super tired this morning, so I drank an energy drink. Maybe that's it," I muttered hoping it was a good enough lie.

"I'm calling an ambulance," Jeff stated.

In severe pain, holding my chest, aware of all the drugs in my system and the expense of an ambulance, I quickly blurted out, "No. Don't call. I'll have my dad take me."

Jeff gave in and advised me to get to a doctor. As I began to call my dad, I thought to myself, *I finally pushed it too far. This is it; I am dying.*

I quickly dialed. "Hey, Dad, I need help. I'm at work, and it feels like I'm having a heart attack."

Worried, but thankfully not drunk, he responded, "Son? Mikey? Okay, son, hang on. I'll be right there."

"Okay, Dad," I said, hanging up the phone and letting the others know my dad was on the way.

He was there in no time and helped me up and into his

car. I couldn't believe that just two weeks ago, he was in my shoes. Panicked on the inside with a calm exterior, he helped carry me into the emergency room.

"So what's going on, Michael?" a nurse asked me.

"I don't know. My heart feels like it's coming out of my chest."

~ ~ ~

Two days later, I was still in the hospital. They had me on a continual IV of fluids and medication, taking blood and running all sorts of tests. My body and brain were exhausted, and I slept for hours on end.

I didn't mind having to stay awhile. In fact, I've always loved hospitals. Being in the hospital is one of the few places I've ever felt safe—the only time where anyone actually took care of me or cared how I was feeling. For me, being in the hospital felt like checking into a spa. It might sound strange, but there's something comforting about being in a place where people die. It was the idea that one day I was going to die and thank God, because I thought I was in this perpetual state of hell for eternity. I would have chats with God when I was in this space. I wasn't sure how to have faith or what faith to follow, but I often found myself praying to God, saying things like, "God, I want to do your will, just show me how to do it. Help me get out of this hell so I can do whatever it is you want me to do." I was desperate.

I was filled to the brim with absolute shame and self-pity. I couldn't believe that nobody came to visit me, not even my cousin Mark, but then again, why would he? He had warned me the night before, and I had completely blown him off.

The doctor walked in, severing my internal dialogue. "Hi, Michael. How's it going?"

"Hi, uh, feeling a little better," I mumbled, knowing full well he had run numerous rounds of blood work on me.

"That's good. That's really good. So...we found cocaine in your system."

I heard him, but I didn't care.

The doctor filled the silence. "That probably had something to do with your heart palpitations."

I quietly managed an "okay."

"You're really lucky; you did have a minor heart attack. It's probably best to get off that stuff and get help if you need it." The doctor said while handing me a pamphlet on rehab and substance abuse programs, similar to what I had just received for my dad.

"Thank you, sir, I'll look into it."

"Take care of yourself," he said as he turned to leave the room.

I said nothing. I just stared off into space—lost.

When I got out of the hospital, I drank.

[SOLANA BEACH, CA —OCTOBER 2008]

I finally decided that it was time to get my shit together. I focused on trying to better my life and to not drink. I didn't have any support, wasn't going to AA or anything like that. I was white-knuckling it, just trying to make it from one day to another without drinking, the way my old man did when he was sober. I was doing everything I could to hold on to my budding surfing career from exercising to doing hot yoga and eating clean. And of course, surfing as much as possible.

Fred was no longer with Zoo York and I had a new team manager, James. James was great; he was a New York surfer with the grit to match. He didn't take shit from anyone but was beyond kind to those he cared about.

One afternoon James called me up. "Mikey boy! How's it going, dude?"

"It's going really well, man, just at work."

"Nice. Well, I'll make this quick. I'm sorry, but we're not gonna renew your contract, and we're gonna have to let you go from the team."

"Ahhh, really, man," I said, completely shattered but at the same time thinking, *Okay, this was a long time coming.*

"Yeah, sorry, you just haven't produced anything in a long time and we gotta keep moving forward." He paused before continuing, "Listen, you're an amazing surfer, and maybe if you work really hard in the next year, we can get you back on the team."

"Oh, okay, I understand, James," I said, somewhat at a loss for words. "Yeah, I'll work hard this year and see if I can get back to a good spot with you guys. Thanks for everything."

Getting dropped from the team hit me harder than I could imagine. It felt surreal in a sense, like having the rug pulled out from under me. I felt like I was finally working on getting my life together and never imagined that it could be too little, too late.

Instead of staying focused and using this as fuel to motivate me to keep getting healthier mentally and physically, I went into yet another self-destructive period. An endless carousel of blackout benders and holing up under my covers for days and weeks on end.

[ENCINITAS, CA —NOVEMBER 2008]

While I was continuing to perfect the art of self-sabotage, Mark was scoring waves and landing higher-paying sponsors. It was all anyone in our small town could talk about. I would be hanging in town with a friend, only to hear another one of my buddies calling out, "Dude, you see Mark's new shot in the mag?"

Shaking my head, "Naw, not yet. Is it sick?"

"Yeah, it's insane. Big backside hack."

"Nice," I said, feeling like I wanted to hide, to disappear altogether.

"Man, he's better than you now, isn't he?"

"I wouldn't say that. Every dog has its day," I fired back, half joking but pissed.

"And he's better looking." Always said with a chuckle.

I was fuming. I did what I could to ignore him, but it was all around me. I walked inside 7-Eleven to grab a beer and picked up the issue with Mark's shot in it. Immediately I was overcome by shame, the humiliation and anger bubbling up from my core. I put the magazine back on the rack and walked out, wondering what had happened to me.

It was never-ending. I would be heading out to surf, the only reprieve I had, and someone would say, "Mark's blowing up, huh? You're living in his shadow now." I couldn't shake it. I was furious, embarrassed, and hurt, but I refused to let anyone see it. Instead, I would just laugh it off.

Not too long ago, I had been hearing things like, "You're a better surfer than Mark; you have a maturity about your surfing that he doesn't have." Not this shit. I wasn't used to hearing that Mark wanted it more than me or that he was one-upping me.

My ego couldn't take it.

I went into my car, snorted some blow, and headed out to surf.

[SEASIDE BEACH, CA —FEBRUARY 2009]

By 2009, I was living in a makeshift shipping container. Not one of those modern container homes that everyone is used to seeing these days. This place was a stand-alone structure in the back of a lawn mower repair shop in town. All it had was a bed, a makeshift closet with a rod, and a shitty desk. There was no kitchen, no toilet, and no shower. I had one of those camping shower bags outside, and that's where I pissed too. If I had to take a shit, I would go to the nearby Starbucks. Eventually, the landlord smelled the urine and gave me keys to a bathroom in the other building. I should have been mortified but I couldn't bring myself to care.

It was three thirty in the afternoon when I heard banging at my door. I was hungover, at rock bottom, and suicidal. Like father like son, I had become a master of self-destruction.

"Mikey, you there?"

"Yeah, I'm here," I said, disheveled, walking over to open the door.

"Hi, son, sorry to bother you. You okay? I was wondering if I could borrow ten dollars. Betsy needs gas; we're on empty."

"I don't have it, Dad. I'm sorry," I said, trying to shake him off so I could get back to bed. "I'm not feeling well. I'm gonna get some rest; I'll call you later."

"Okay, son," he said, turning away from the door in defeat.

Here I was completely hopeless, with my dad knocking on the door to borrow ten dollars. Demoralized, I got back in bed with the all-too-familiar thought that I needed a massive change or I was going to die.

[SEASIDE BEACH, CA —MAY 2009]

Thankfully, God handed me a life raft.

They say that God gives you what you need, whether it be people or experiences, when you need them. Or in my case, when you're finally willing to listen.

I was checking the surf and ran into my good friend Noah. Noah was a year older than me and a big influence on my life. He was someone I had always looked up to and admired. He was insanely talented and was one of those guys who could have had the world by the balls, if he'd had his shit together.

Noah was a good-looking guy with dark hair that contrasted against his fair, freckled skin.

He was more active than most of the people I knew and was always seeking adventure. Noah was also a bit eccentric, highly intelligent, and quick-witted. There was something about him that was disturbed in a way. Even he wondered at times if he might be schizophrenic.

"Hey, Noah, how have you been?" I asked, thinking to myself that he looked better than he'd looked in ages. "I haven't seen you."

"Yeah, I've been doing a little better. I've been sober for ninety days," Noah said, with an ease about him.

"No way! Really? How did you do that?" I asked with both curiosity and respect.

"I've been going to AA meetings. I realized I'm an alcoholic."

"Holy shit, wow," I said, shocked by how candidly he revealed this to me. His honesty gave me the space to continue, "I've been in such a bad way. I can't stop drinking. I'm in a really dark place."

"I know, man," he said, fully aware of the state I was in. Hell, he was in it not too long ago. "If you want to come to a meeting sometime, you're always welcome."

In that moment, something shifted in me.

It was as if it were suddenly okay for me to admit to myself, to admit to others, that I was an alcoholic.

"Okay, thanks, man. I need to do something. I'm not kidding, I'm gonna die."

~ ~ ~

The next day I found myself at Morgan's house. I was in such a raw space and needed to be around people who were supportive. When you're on the road to sobriety, you figure out really quickly who is going to support you versus who is going to continue encouraging old habits. You also realize that the people you've been spending most of your time with usually have three options if they continue on their paths: jails, institutions, or death. Unfortunately, I know people who ended up in all three of these camps.

I was inside with Morgan working on repairing the dings in a couple of our boards when I got a call from Ari's grandma, Em. Em was an amazing woman. She was in her nineties and was equal parts sweet and witty. This woman had seen it all. She was fiercely independent, divorced forty years earlier when it was really not common, and supported herself and her family as a social worker.

The moment I saw her name come up on the screen of my phone, I knew something was off. Instinctually I think I knew exactly why she was calling.

With concern and compassion, I picked up. "Hi, Em."

Distressed, she replied, "Hi, Mike. I have some terrible news." She paused, collecting herself. "Ari's dead. They found him on the beach in front of Jack's house in Bali."

"What?" I asked, fully aware of what she said but my mind refusing to process.

It's surreal to get news like this, news that one of your best friends has killed themself. No matter what, no matter how bad the addiction or depression, you're never prepared for it. Your mind just doesn't follow along.

"Yes, he OD'd," she said, pausing to collect herself. "They think he did it on purpose. He said goodbye to his brother before he walked out to the beach and passed."

Later we came to learn that he mixed Xanax and Oxycontin, a known combination in the drug world as a way to commit suicide.

I tried to visualize this scene in my mind and rationalize the Ari I grew up with against this version of him. The Ari I knew when we were younger was so full of life.

I was pulled back by Em's voice. "I just wanted you to

know. I feel so terrible, Mike. I'm going to go now, but you take care of yourself and come see me. Speak soon."

"Okay, Em. Goodbye," I said in disbelief.

Again, my mind wandered to imagining Ari. His curly blond hair, bright blue eyes, and his tan skin. He had a wisdom beyond his years, was the ultimate storyteller, and despite the pain he carried, he was a kind soul. The Ari I knew laughed a lot, but it was clear that he was living with some sort of turmoil from within, a discomfort in the world.

That day, the day of Ari's passing, May 7, 2009, is my sobriety date.

[SEASIDE BEACH, CA —MAY 2009]

Two days after I bumped into Noah, and the day after I received news of Ari's death, I was sitting in my first AA meeting at the Community Center at Eden Gardens Park.

I had no idea what to expect. For so long I held on to these preconceived notions of what AA was going to be like. I was wrong on so many levels.

I remember my eyes welling up with tears as an AA member detailed their experience with incredible strength and hope. Immediately I felt an overwhelming sense of relief. It was as if a huge weight was lifted off my shoulders and I finally figured out what was wrong with me.

I am an alcoholic.

I had less than zero money, so I had to detox myself. All I did was go to AA meetings and then go back to my glorified shipping container. Some call this poor man's rehab. Withdrawal symptoms kicked in after day one. I was shaking, nauseous, anxious, and on the verge of a panic attack at all times. I could hardly sleep, tossing and turning all night. My version of yoga. I was hallucinating and confused. I must have had high blood pressure because my heart was racing and beating heavily for days. When I had the appetite, I would count change and go get two tacos for ninety-nine cents at Jack in the Box. No one knew how bad it was. People might have known it was bad, but my ego wouldn't let them know how much I was truly hurting. Toward the end of my drinking, I had the shakes so bad that I could barely write my name, although I had no clue it had anything to do with alcohol. I thought I was dealing with early onset of arthritis or Parkinson's. I didn't fuckin' know. It wasn't until I was three weeks to one month sober that I could sign my name again and realized the shakes were from alcohol.

After spending so much time working in rehabs and sober livings since getting sober, I now see how insane it was that I detoxed myself in that shithole. When I tell people in recovery my story, they are in disbelief. I didn't even know I was doing it tough at the time. I was just doing what I had to do. I constantly see people in rehabs who complain about the facility they're in or the detox program they went through, and I have to hold my tongue. Most of the time, these people are being pampered with nice meals, a sauna and spa, and a beautiful rehabilitation center—all while wearing a white robe in addition to having their own personal nurse standing by. It's sad to say, but most of the time these people don't stay sober. They say the odds of someone staying sober after rehab are 8 to12 percent.

I now look back on what I went through as a blessing. If you really want to get sober, you can do it, no matter what the circumstance. I've seen so many people go through recovery and not stay sober because their families enable them. They never hit true rock bottom because their families smother them with support. Sometimes the best thing you can do is to let someone rot in hell, like I did. It's a big gamble though, because they could die. At a certain point, you can only do so much though. A person has to want to get sober for themself. If they don't, you're wasting your time. Like my dad always said, live and let live, kid.

~ ~ ~

Ten days into my sobriety, I heard a passage in the Big Book of Alcoholics Anonymous that resonated with me in a way few things ever had. It was at a big men's stag meeting, with close to 150 men in attendance.

The room was quiet when the man read page 558 from the Big Book, starting with "All these things and many, many more, A.A. gave me. But above all, it taught me how to handle sobriety," and ending at the bottom of page 559.

This passage hit me harder than anything else in the early days of my sobriety. I can't even remember how many times I had stood in the bar, belligerent, thinking that I was going to be exalted to some position of power and prestige. I was coming to terms with how delusional I was. It was like entering a new dimension of existence, one that was based in humility, and truth be told, I didn't like it very much, but at least it was real.

Beyond reading the Big Book and having a set speaker, I had no idea how the format of big meetings went before I went to my first one. When they asked newcomers to introduce themselves at the beginning of the meeting, I raised my hand, having no idea that they would later call me to the front podium and have me introduce myself to the whole group. I would never have raised my hand if I had known that was the case.

I made my way to the front of the room and positioned myself at the podium.

"Mike, alcoholic," I said.

Everything after that is a sort of a blur. I had never done any public speaking in my life, and this was a big and intimidating group of about 150 rowdy men. When I was younger, I used sarcasm to deal with being shy or uncomfortable, and so I did the same thing here. At the end of my scattered share, I said something like, "I'm ten days sober, and my goal is to get ten years sober and then start drinking again." I was joking but clearly, I was the only one who found it funny. The whole room was crickets. These guys are kind and fun-loving, really a good group, but they took their sobriety very seriously.

It was life or death for these guys, and come to find out, it was for me too.

I wrapped up my share, and they applauded me like they do every share. I sat down and listened for the rest of the meeting. I later learned not to drink so much coffee before the meeting, just in case I was called up to share again.

The incredible thing that I learned during this meeting was that these guys were able to have a good time. They all had a great sense of humor despite my failed attempt at making them laugh. They got their lives on track, but they didn't lose their personality. And, they were sober.

[SEASIDE BEACH, CA —JUNE 2009]

My approach to getting sober was no different than how I approach everything else in life: it was all or nothing. I went through the Twelve Steps within one to two weeks but was making the first round of amends for a good six months. Some amends I was able to tackle immediately, whereas others revealed themselves to me in years to come, and then there are the living amends, which I will be doing for the rest of my life.

Going through the Twelve Step program is a life-changing process. For me, the most powerful steps were 5 and 9. Step 5 requires admittance of our wrongs to God, to ourselves, and to another person—in my case, to my first sponsor. My first sponsor was a temporary sponsor, which is common. It allows you to get the ball rolling with a sponsor that is "good enough" but might not be the person you click with on a multitude of levels. For me, it was all about getting through the early stages of sobriety, familiarizing myself with the steps, and embarking on the journey of Recovery.

Through Step 5, I was able to tell someone things I never planned on telling anyone, ever. Like many people do, I left things out the first time I did my Fifth step. I was scared and embarrassed. Not being completely honest ate at me. Later that night, I was home, sitting with my thoughts, and I knew that if I couldn't be completely honest, I was going to drink.

I texted my sponsor and said, *Hey, I have something else I need to tell you. Can we meet again tomorrow?*

He responded, *Of course.*

I went to bed that night walking through what I left out.

There was a rumor going around town that I had an illegitimate kid. I had no idea if this was true or not, but I had slept with a girl while I was in a blackout and later learned that she had a child. The story I heard was that she wasn't sure who the father was; it was either me or some Portuguese fella, and she didn't really care either way. She was determined to raise the child on her own.

The idea of having a child at this point in my life filled me with more than just fear; it was absolute terror. First of all, I wanted nothing to do with the girl I slept with. It wasn't that she was a bad person, I just didn't like her, let alone love her. I had slept with her because I was drunk and she was willing, period. Second, I was barely hanging on as it was. My parents were still homeless, and I was living in a container with no bathroom. My money situation was in the red with late fees stacking up month after month. Bringing a child into the world in that space, physically and emotionally, was far from optimal.

In my mind, I was convinced the child was mine, in part because a friend of hers told me the child looked like me.

I couldn't handle it, and so I didn't.

I was a coward. I ignored it and drank myself half to death night after night.

It was more than the fear of being a father to this woman's child. Each time I drank, I did my best to forget about the problems I created by creating new problems. The new problems would always drown out the old, and I created a constant cycle of turmoil.

So, in my second crack at doing Step 5, as honestly as possible, I told my sponsor the 100 percent truth, not 98 percent, and here's what he said:

"Okay, well, guess what?" he said with a reassuring calmness to him. "The same thing happened to me. The kid is nine now, and I'm very present in his life. It turned out to be a great thing."

He paused, letting it sink in for a moment.

"And guess what else? You need to contact the mom when the time is right, and get a paternity test."

That was it; I said my deepest secret out loud and it wasn't met with the slightest bit of judgment. Instead, it was met with compassion and a direct solution, which was new for me. For a few moments, I felt the weight of the world lifting. Massive relief filled my soul. There was still a lot of work to be done, but I felt like there was a clear path.

If I took the next step laid out in front of me, one foot in front of the other as they say, things would be okay.

When the time was right, I reached out to the woman I had slept with. It took me a solid year to be able to get there, but through the help of my first long-term sponsor, I was able to dial her number. Without any resistance, she agreed to have a paternity test done. She also revealed to me that she was sober and was also in the process of working through the Twelve Steps.

What are the odds?

By the time we got the test back, I was at peace with whatever the results were.

I was not the father.

There I was, drinking over something, for years, that wasn't even true.

~ ~ ~

When I made it to Step 9, I had the chance to make things right with people I hadn't spoken to in years. There are many people that I had to make amends with; an example of this was my friend Jason and his family.

After I tried to take Jason's parents' Chevy the night I got jumped at The Gym, things got pretty sour between us. I was so ashamed of doing something that stupid that I couldn't bring myself to show my face around their house. What if I had actually taken their car? What if I killed someone while drunk?

These were people that I had seen almost every day for years. I was so embarrassed by my actions that I just stopped talking to them.

I reached out to Jason's dad and asked if he had time to talk. He said yes and invited me over to his place. I made amends for my behavior and asked if there was anything I could do to make things right. He seemed to really respect my being there, my owning up to my mistakes and making amends. He shared with me that he battled addiction in the past, which was surprising to me because he seemed to be so together.

These are a couple of small examples of how the program was beginning to shape my life. For the first time, I was taking responsibility for my actions and trying to make changes, rather than running away or hiding. None of this was my idea; I can't take any credit for it.

It's all the power of the program of Alcoholics Anonymous.

[SOLANA BEACH, CA —JANUARY 2010]

A few years earlier, before I left for Australia and before I got sober, I had sold my car. When I came back, I was a mess and was in no place to be able to buy another car. For a good six to eight months I had no car, which is pretty challenging in California. I was skating everywhere, and I was drunk and doing drugs most of the time.

At the time, Ari was also struggling pretty badly. He had just left the most recent of the California rehab centers and was headed back to Bali. Before leaving, he asked me if I wanted to buy his car. I told him I did, but that I didn't have the money right now. Ari was fine with it. He told me to just give him what I had and that I could give him the rest later. I gave him about $1,500 in cash with a promise to pay him an additional $1,500 when I had the money.

That was it. Ari got on a plane back to Bali, and I never saw him again.

When I got sober, I knew I needed to get my life together. There was no support coming from anywhere. I needed to do this on my own. I was lucky enough to still have Ari's car and to have been able to hold on to my job as an ocean lifeguard. At the time, I saw that firefighters had really good lives; they made good money, had a nice schedule where they still had the freedom to surf, and were able to provide for a family.

Being an ocean lifeguard for the past six years gave me a good introduction to the guys. I started doing ride-alongs with firemen at various San Diego fire departments. I was even able to enroll in an EMT Paramedic Prep Course, which might sound easy, but it's actually considered to be a pretty difficult course. There is so much to learn about the human body, about what it really takes to be a first responder. They take it very seriously because they know the weight of having someone's life in their hands. One of the guys in the class with me had just finished college. He had gotten his degree and told me that this course was harder than anything he had taken during his four years of college.

I gave it everything I had. I stayed sober for the full course, an entire semester. I put everything I had into it, but also I was really struggling with studying. I didn't know it at the time but my brain was in a mixed state of healing through sobriety while also wrestling with ADHD.

You have to get an 80 percent or higher to pass the course and I got a 78 percent. I failed. I failed the class even though I was sober. I was demoralized, close to flat broke, and had absolutely no idea what I was going to do.

I leaned into recovery, going to AA meetings, and connecting with my sponsor. Thankfully, I had a sponsor who had become like a father to me. AA became like a family, a family that was beginning to raise me and still is, even to this day.

During this time, I continued to talk to Ari's dad, Jack. Ari had left a gaping hole in our hearts, and we stayed in touch, checking in on each other the best we could.

I told Jack about what I was going through and how I was struggling to find my path here. I also told him about how I still owed Ari for the car. I knew Jack had been the one who bought the car in the first place, so I really felt like I owed him the balance; I just didn't have it.

I couldn't believe how he responded when I told him I didn't have the money. "Mike, don't worry about paying me for the car. Take whatever money you have and buy yourself a plane ticket and come visit me. I want to see you here in Bali."

Jack became like a father to me, and I became a son to him. The son he lost, the father I lost in many ways, who was still alive but wasn't present because of alcoholism among many other things.

Jack inviting me to Bali ended up being another new beginning for me. It gave me something to focus on after failing the firefighter exam. My goal was to save enough money to take care of some things at home and buy a ticket to Bali.

[ENCINITAS, CA —MARCH 2010]

I was sound asleep when my phone started ringing. It was about 1:00 a.m., and it dawned on me that in the past I would have been out partying at this hour. Instead, I had been sleeping soundly for the past few hours.

I looked over and saw it was Mark. I hadn't been spending much time with him lately because I was sober and he was still drinking. The last time I hung out with him, he was drunk and needed a ride. He kept asking me to take him to the liquor store even though he was already drunk. What I observed in that moment was that there was no not getting more alcohol; it wasn't an option, and that's different from the normal drinker. It was an eye-opening experience to see the alcoholic at work.

I answered the phone. "Yo, what's up?" I asked, immediately aware of his crying on the other end.

Sobbing rapidly, without taking a breath, "Mike, can you come get me? I almost just killed myself. I was standing in front of the train and jumped outta the way at the last second. Please come get me. I'm near E Street and the train tracks." He finally exhaled and I heard him gasp for air between the sobs.

"Holy shit Mark...okay. I'll come get you. Hold on, I'll be right there."

I quickly got into my car, well aware of the fact that this was becoming a family pattern. My nerves were firing during the ten-minute drive to get him. I had this mixed feeling of nervousness met with excitement over the idea of him hitting a point where he wanted to get sober. That doesn't mean I wished him a rock bottom in the sense that I wished him pain, but recently I saw his drinking and drug use destroying him day by day, and I wished him a path of recovery.

When I finally reached Mark, he was still crying.

"You alright?" I asked, knowing he clearly wasn't.

"I'm just tired of this shit. I can't handle it anymore."

Not asking any questions, I just told him, "I know. It's alright. I'm here. Let's go home."

"I took some pingers tonight that made me go really low, and I decided to go to the train tracks and end it. I jumped outta the way at the last moment."

"Holy shit. Okay, I'm here," I said, putting my hand on his shoulder. "Hang in there; you're gonna be alright."

A year later Mark would yet again follow in my footsteps, only this time, in deciding to get sober.

~ ~ ~

Between Ari and Mark, there were too many memories here. Too many failures, too much regret, and too many old friends who were accustomed to my bad behavior. Later that year, just around when I hit one year of sobriety, I made the decision to leave California. I was following the encouragement Jack instilled in me. The feeling that I could travel the world and experience new places, cultures, and people with my own eyes, the same way he had. I was feeling really good, healthy, and fit, the best I had in ages, and you could tell just by looking at me.

My parents, however, were still struggling. They were posted up in a Motel 6 just outside of town. I knew it wasn't going to be easy, but I was already committed to leaving, and I was dropping by their hotel room to let them know. At this point, my goal was to leave and go from Japan to Indonesia to visit Jack. I had no return date in mind.

There was a silence in the room after I told them. A lack of understanding why I would want to do this, why I would want to start clean in a new place.

"I love you guys, but I have to do this."

"Really, son, are you sure? It's so far away," my dad said almost like I was abandoning them.

"I'm sure; this is something I have to do. There's something pulling me out there."

My mom was heartbroken, but she knew I had made my decision. "Okay, son. We love you," she said, tearing up. "Please be safe and call us as much as possible."

"I will. I'll be okay. I am worried about you guys." Taking a moment to find a balance of concern, compassion, and pressure, I said, "Please try and get sober."

I hugged both my parents tightly, said goodbye, and got in the car.

Pops and I, age 1 ½

Second grade. Kona, Big Island.

Mom and I, age eleven

My new whip. Senior year high school.

Lower Trestles, California, age seventeen

Prom, age eighteen

Friend of Dad's and I in front of the mattress store

Local Profile

Mike Millin, Solana Beach

Age: **19**
Hometown: **Solana Beach**
Favorite Surfers: **Andy Irons, Taj Burrow, Rob Machado**
Favorite Spot: **Seaside**
Sponsors: **Aaron Chang clothing, Sanuk sandals, Xcel wetsuits, Mitch's surf shop, UM surfboards**

UG: What have you been up to lately?
MM: I've just been surfing a lot. Mostly just around here. Yesterday I helped Aaron Chang move stuff from one warehouse to another. They're moving into a bigger warehouse in Carlsbad. They just outgrew that little warehouse in Oceanside.

UG: I heard they have some new investors. What are the plans, do you know?
MM: They're coming out with a new line of clothing and expanding. They're getting into a lot of different kinds of stores.

UG: What else is going on?
I'm saving up to go to Hawaii this winter. The north shore. Aaron's going to help cover some of the costs, but I have to help out. I used to live in Kauai and I have a bunch of friends over there on Kauai. But I want to try out the north shore. I haven't been there yet. Aaron has a house on Sunset Beach.

UG: How about contests? Do you surf in a lot of contests?
MM: Last year I did the ISF high school series. I got second place overall for the season. I did the Volcom VQS series and qualified for the championships up in Newport. That was a cool contest. They had gambling for the kids. They start you out with $100 in Volcom chips and there was this big gambling area for surfers to hang out in between heats. You could play for shoes, backpacks, grip pads, leashes and stuff. And there were guys there from Florida and Japan and Australia and all over. I was stoked I qualified for it.

Local Profile by UnderGround Media, age eighteen
UnderGround Media, 2003, photo by Cooper and Sean Wesley

Rocky Point, Hawaii. Full page ad *Surfing Magazine*, age nineteen
Issue: *Surfing Magazine*, May 2004

Carlsbad, California

Self-destruct mode, right before getting sober, age twenty-four

First landing in Bali

Sanuk ad van collage, age twenty-five

Monkeys in Bali

Bingin, Bali

Bingin, Bali

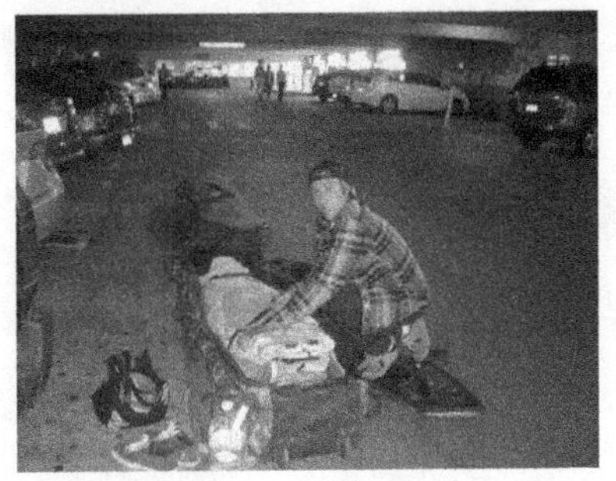

Packing surfboards at LAX before heading to Japan with $200 to my name

Tokyo, Japan

Having some fun with the people of Japan

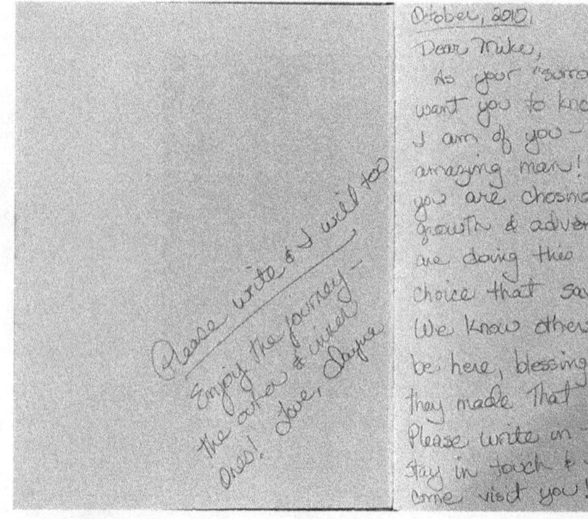

October, 2010,

Dear Mike,

As your "surrogate mom," I want you to know how proud I am of you – you are an amazing man! Every day, you are chosing "LIFE", love, growth & adventure. You are doing this from a sober choice that saved your life. We know others who would be here, blessing our lives, if they made that same choice. Please write in this journal – stay in touch & I hope to come visit you! I love you honey, so much!

Please write & I will too

Enjoy the journey – the outer & inner ones! Love, Dayna

Letter of encouragement from the mom of one of my best friends

Lakey Peak. Sumbawa, Indonesia.

Lakey Peak. Sumbawa, Indonesia.

My crew back home sent me a signed surfboard while I was working in the mines in Australia.

Supersucks. West Sumbawa, Indonesia.

Mentawais, Indonesia

Padang Padang, Bali

[TOKYO, JAPAN —APRIL 2010]

It's funny, I never thought I would make it to Japan. It was always such a massive, but also unrealistic, dream for me. No one who I knew personally had ever been there, and it was one of those places that just seemed so exotic to me. There are many countries that I felt this way about. I remember thinking as a young man that if I traveled to these countries, I would have made it. It was almost like if I could get there, I would be set for life, and I would finally feel accomplished. Throughout my life, traveling has led to some amazing experiences. I am grateful that I did it, and I did it my way. What I have come to learn after traveling the world is that I am still unfulfilled. It didn't solve everything for me, and I think it must be a similar experience to making massive amounts of money.

Japan was the starting place for me to commit to leaving home and experiencing the world for myself. In the past, I was always doing short trips where I knew I had to come back home to immense struggle. This was different. I was sober, and I had no plans to return to California, no timeline I had to stick to, and no boss that I had to answer to. I knew that by the time I got to Bali, my cost of living would be minimal. I could stay with Jack as long as I needed, rent a motorbike, and just see what happened. I packed up my two board bags, otherwise known as board coffins, with five boards in each bag. The airline didn't bat an eye. They charged me $75 for the extra board bag and I was on my way. I arrived during Japan's cherry blossom season, one of the best times of the year. The trees are so beautiful that they look animated. They have a certain glow to them—an incredible white and purple glow. I was blown away by the thousands of Japanese people who were flocking to the parks during this time of year to have picnics.

I was staying with a friend, Aiko, at the time. I met him years ago in San Diego while out surfing, and we stayed in touch. Aiko was a character. He was a great host, incredibly kind and welcoming. He was a small guy, about five foot three with the biggest smile. While I was newly sober, Aiko absolutely loved to drink alcohol. I joined him and my crew of Japanese friends. They all spoke minimal English but we never had any problems. No problems, other than Aiko being a bit cheeky, teaching me some Japanese.

Aiko told me that when I meet someone for the first time I should say, "Hajimemashite, watashinonamaeha maikudesu, watashi wa geidesu." This means, "Hello, nice to meet you, my name is Mike, and I am gay." At the time, I wasn't exactly sure what it meant, but I had an idea it was something along these lines. I had a lot of fun walking around introducing myself to people in Tokyo. Some people would laugh instantly; others were a bit confused, which provided its own form of humor for me.

The people were really incredible. They stood out to me, and they still do. They were so humble and hospitable, so nice, probably the nicest people I have met anywhere in the world. Japan is up there as one of my favorite countries. I honestly considered moving there. The land is beautiful, and the authentic Japanese food is my favorite. I can't even remember half of the things that I ate, but I remember it being cold during that time of year and the food warming my soul. Everything from Japanese curry and barbecues to ramen. One meal I vividly recall was eating raw horse meat dipped in raw egg. Sounds disgusting, right? Well, it was, but in Japan, this is a delicacy. You wouldn't believe how expensive that meal was. I only had the privilege of experiencing it because my buddy Aiko's parents were wealthy and took us to a special dinner one night because they had wanted to meet me. It was incredibly generous of them and speaks to the character of his parents but also the people in general.

I had so many experiences in Japan, which says a lot considering I arrived in Japan with $200 to my name. Nobody knew this. I didn't want to stress anyone out, but also, I really didn't want anyone to know how broke I was. I was able to budget $200 for the first couple of days before finding a surf shop that agreed to buy eight of my ten surfboards. Aiko and I stood in this shop, him translating back and forth as I tried to make a deal.

"How much is 340,000 yen?" I asked.

Aiko turned to the store owner, translated, and then turned back to me. "It's about $3,000 USD."

"Okay, let's do it," I said. "Tell her we have a deal and thank her for me."

I can't tell you the relief I felt once I was able to sell those boards. Money isn't everything, but it sure is a factor in life.

I still had two boards for myself, and trust me, I got plenty of use out of them. When people think of Japan, they don't typically think about surfing, but there are some great spots if you're willing to pay to get to them. I headed to the coastal town of Chiba. I couldn't believe the toll costs to get to the beach from Tokyo. It averaged $100!

I surfed in front of the Fukushima power plant months before the massive tsunami hit. I remember watching it live. I had never seen anything so horrific in my life. The streets I had driven down, the beaches I had walked on to go surfing, all of it under a massive wall of debris and water. I remember watching people driving for their lives only to be swallowed by the wall of water.

My friends took me out to a club in the city one night. Tokyo is probably the biggest city I've ever experienced. They have fourteen downtown areas, each one the size of Times Square in New York. Massive. At this point, I hadn't spoken to anyone who spoke English fluently in a while, and I was starting to feel a little lonely. The Japanese club was full of Japanese people, obviously, but in the distance, I saw a white woman. I thought I had to go talk to her just to have a "normal" conversation with someone. By this point, I was so exhausted from speaking broken English with everyone I met.

I walked up to the girl and said, "Hello," with a smile.

She looked at me, confused, and said, "No English," while waving her arms across her body.

It was the first time I saw a white person who was Asian. I know it's common to meet Asian people who were born and raised in the States that don't speak their native tongue, but this completely threw me off. She was a white chick who was born and raised in Japan. She even moved like a Japanese person, in how she spoke, her facial expression, and her body language.

I did my best to say thank you, have a good night, and went on my way.

Being in Tokyo felt like I was in the future. My friends were paying for their items with their phones, and this was way before anyone in the States had any clue this was possible. I slept in a capsule hotel that was set up like a morgue. That makes it sound scary but it wasn't. It was actually pretty comfortable. For $30 I had my own little capsule with a TV, some storage, and all the amenities I needed with a communal shower at the end of the hall. It's such a strange contrast to the surrounding towns filled with ancient temples. I remember stopping by a beach in one of the villages. There were no waves but thousands of people out with their surfboards. They just sat on their boards in the water. I guess they just wanted to act like they were surfing.

My time in Japan was really special for me. I was so in love with the idea of traveling and experiencing new cultures. I knew this was just the beginning for me, but at some point during my time in Tokyo, I hurt my wrist. I ended up going back to LA to earn some extra money and deal with my wrist. In the process, I picked up some more surfboards to sell in Japan before my first trip to Indonesia.

[DEL MAR, CA —APRIL 2011]

I was sitting in the backyard of the house I knew so well. It wasn't my house, it was Ari's, but I felt so comfortable here that it might as well have been mine. There's something about your best friend's house; when you look back it just feels like a home away from home.

Jack was visiting from Bali and I couldn't wait to catch up with him. Jack is, and always was, such a character. He had to be close to sixty-five at this point but is one of those guys who aged really well, and he knows it too. We joked that he never met a mirror he didn't like. He was eccentric and a rebel, picking up and moving to Bali at a time when nobody was doing it. He was all about creating his own path, but man he would go out of his way to disagree with you, even if he knew you were right. He's a really great guy, but you absolutely cannot talk to him about spirituality or religion. He thinks anyone who believes in some sort of a God is an idiot, and he is arrogant enough to let you know that.

It was great being able to spend time with Jack. There was something really special about being able to reminisce about Ari and to have Jack's support. I remember thinking, *This is what it feels like to have a father or father figure who actually cared to check in with me*. It was different from my sponsor, who was always helping me stay on the right path. Jack was encouraging me to seek adventure and to experience the fruits of life.

"So whatta you been up to, Mike?"

"Ahhh, not much. I'm managing a sober living in Cardiff. I've really just been doing what I can to help my parents, but you know how it is, they're still struggling," I said knowing full well I could be completely honest.

"Good one, Mike. That's good you can be there for them." He paused for a moment, almost as if he was imagining my reaction before he spoke. "On another note, you want to go on a boat trip?"

I couldn't control the smile planted across my face as my ears immediately perked up. "A boat trip?"

"Yeah, we're gonna go from Sumba to Timor. It's a really magical part of Indonesia. Totally uncrowded waves."

"Wow, Jack, that sounds incredible. I don't know if I'm really in a position to do it right now." I drifted off in thought, wondering how I could possibly turn this down. "I'll have to ask my work if I can get some time off."

"Yeah, Mike. Let me know. I've got a spot for ya."

I managed to get time off work and booked myself a round-trip ticket to join Jack.

As I walked off the plane in Bali, I was suddenly transported back in time to 1993. I was nine years old, and I was walking away from my mom to get on a plane. At the time, we had been living in Hawaii for two to three years while my mom was with Jerry. He was addicted to pills among other things and had a handful of kids of his own. My mom had no money and was not able to financially, or emotionally, take care of herself or me. She had decided she was going to send me to live with my dad back in California. I remember us both crying hysterically as we said goodbye at the airport.

"It's gonna be okay, Michael. I love you," she said to me.

"I love you, Mom," I said, head down as I walked through the gate onto the plane.

Tears ran down my face as I took my seat, looking out the plane window at my mom.

"It's going to be okay; I'm here," a flight attendant said to me, doing her best to comfort me.

I kept looking at the one photograph I had of my dad during the flight. I know my dad had been around when I was younger. He was there from the time I was born to somewhere around three before spending a couple of years in and out. I was so young that I really didn't have any memory of him. It wasn't a nice feeling not knowing who my dad was or feeling like he didn't know me at all. At that age, all you want to know is that your dad cares about you, that he knows who you are. I was nervous but also so excited to meet my dad.

I held the photograph of my dad in my hands, studying it as I walked off the plane into Los Angeles International Airport. I finally saw him. The first thought I had when I saw him was, *Wow, this guy has a massive head, and it's really bright red, like this pink-red, massive head.* I remember being this little kid and being like *Wow, I've never really seen a head like that before.*

"Mikey! It's Papa!"

Speechless, I walked over to my dad.

"I'm so glad you're here, son. Come on, follow me. We're gonna get outta here."

We got in the car and drove north to Oxnard, California, where my dad had gotten sober. I think he was a year or two sober at that point and was living with a good friend of my grandpa's. He was kind enough to let us stay with him, but that meant we were sleeping on a pad on the floor of his living room. This guy used to smoke three packs of cigarettes a day, throwing the butts off the balcony at squirrels.

Completely lost in my memories, as I stepped off the plane. I was jolted back to reality as I heard Jack scream my name.

[UBUD, INDONESIA —APRIL 2011]

Jack gave me a place to call home, and I felt myself experiencing and enjoying life for the first time in as long as I could remember. Not long into the trip, I ran into this guy Darren who I knew from home. It's crazy to be on the other side of the world and bump into someone you know, but that's the thing about surfing: it brings so many people together. Even to this day, I run into people I know from surfing, all over the world.

Darren had spent about seven seasons in Indonesia, for six months at a time, and had the place completely wired. He was one of the most insane underground surfers I ever met. He surfed better than most pros I've seen out in heavy conditions in Indonesia. I have major respect for him; he never had a sponsor and he didn't want one. He surfed for himself, for the love of it, and I learned a lot from him in that.

Even after so many seasons under his belt, Darren was still down to explore. We had this untapped drive for adventure. We'd take motorbikes out and island-hop on ferries in search of new waves in uncharted areas. We rode through small villages, the dirt roads contrasting against the vibrant green jungle. There's a feeling of freedom when you're able to travel around a country for so cheap that it feels like it's free. We would pull up to a warung, an Indonesian version of a restaurant that looks like a hut on the side of the road. We would get these dishes that consisted of a hard-boiled egg, vegetables, and a scoop of rice for 3,000 rupiah, which was about thirty cents USD. Bali is predominantly Hindu, but as you get to these outer islands, Islam becomes the main religion. Some people in the States are fearful of this, but the people are actually incredibly kind, peaceful, and welcoming.

Between the island-hopping and surfing, I joined Jack on the boat trip that got me out to Indonesia in the first place. It was better than I imagined. We took a flight from Bali down to Sumba, where we boarded the boat. The boat was an old wooden sailing yacht that had recently been refurbished while maintaining a feeling of nostalgia. The cabin had five small bedrooms, each with a bunk bed, a full kitchen with a dining table, and a lounge. I spent most of the time on the deck, perched on the bow of the ship, eyes fixed on the horizon. When we traveled across big stretches of open water, we mostly used the motor, but when there was enough wind, the crew would open up the sails, making it feel like we were gliding on the water. I remember looking up and seeing these huge sails working with the wind to move this massive craft. It made me think about the way people used to travel the world, going from place to place with nothing but the sails. It also made me think about how fortunate we were to be on this trip, eating fresh fish, rice, and vegetables every day in between surfing perfect empty waves.

In most areas of Indonesia, empty waves with no other

surfers or boats around is a rarity. We didn't see one other boat for the entire trip. The captain came across as an early pioneer. He was an experienced Australian surfer and had mapped out all the best spots, setting anchor for one to two days until the swell died or we got our fill, and then it was on to the next spot. Every day we surfed our brains out, only taking breaks to come in for meals.

It was the most alive I had ever felt. I never knew that I could feel this alive in sobriety.

Going to Bali was one of the most amazing times I had ever had—and drinking was the furthest thing from my mind. Through that trip, I found a new version of myself. Jack called me the young adventurer; it sparked this passion for seeing the world with my own eyes, which is something I always wanted to do, and it was all because of the new beginning that Jack gave me.

I knew there was no going back to living in California after this. I mean, I had to go back to wrap things up, save up some money, and give my job notice, but there was no way I was staying any longer than I had to. I felt like I was just getting started. There were so many places I still had to go, so many cultures I wanted to experience, and yes, so many waves I wanted to surf.

[PAPUA —DECEMBER 2011]

Nine months later, I officially moved to Bali. When I arrived, I hit up Darren. He couldn't believe my divine timing. He and a couple of his buddies were getting ready to head over to Papua, the Indonesian side of Papua New Guinea. The whole trip was planned by Darren's Portuguese friend Henry. Henry was another underground surfer that Darren had met in the Mentawais. He had been looking at this place on Google Earth for a couple of years and said this spot had the potential to be as good as the Mentawais, except that nobody knew about it.

Darren insisted that I join them, and I was more than happy to. Immediately upon landing in Bali, I got all my stuff together and jumped on this trip to Papua with Darren, Henry, and a group of guys I hadn't met yet. The trip ended up being another highlight of my surf travels, something I will never forget. As the small prop plane was landing in Papua, I had this raw feeling of fear and adventure. Part of the fear stemmed from the fact that Papua was actively tribal and it was reported that cannibalism was still practiced. The thrill of adventure far outweighed the fear. We had just taken a leap of faith and were screaming with excitement at the idea of entering the unknown.

We were in Papua for two or three weeks. We rented motorbikes in the main town, building our own surf racks out of bamboo and twine to put on the sides. In Bali, it was no big deal to rent a motorbike with surf racks, but there were no surfers in Papua, so we made these janky bamboo racks and grabbed some supplies we needed in town. From there, we started to make our way to the northern coast, which is the Pacific Ocean in Indonesia. It's actually really rare; most people think of Indonesia in the Indian Ocean, but this was the Pacific side that gets typhoon swells coming from areas like Japan and Taiwan.

When we arrived on the north coast, we were surprised to see remnants of the military from World War II. A lot of people don't know this, and we didn't at the time either, but Papua New Guinea served as a midpoint between opposing armies in the early 1940s. By 1945, the north coast and the surrounding islands experienced excessive bombings and wreckage largely at the hands of Japan. In addition to the military wreckage, I was surprised to see that the people looked African. They looked black, but they spoke Indonesian, and they would salute you. They saw us driving past, realized we were white, and would stop and salute us like they were in the military. The remnants of World War II were all still there, which we thought was really interesting and was not something we had ever seen before.

When we arrived at the small shack we rented, we set up mosquito nets and set out to scout the area. We scoped the areas that Henry had seen on Google Earth. The place had a similar feel to the Mentawais both in the insane breaks and in how tropical it looked.

We found a mechanical left that was like Bingin in Bali, which is a barreling playful left. We also came across this other reef that breaks like a beach break that was really rip-able, along with another point with crazy potential, knowing that if a big swell hit it would be similar to Nias.

During the trip, I got to know these characters that had joined us. In addition to Darren and Henry, we were accompanied by Walt and Rowan. Walt was this fifty-two-year-old man who happened to be from my hometown in North County San Diego. He had a drug deal go bad in Encinitas in the '80s before he ran away and never went home. He was on the run and really fried from drugs and alcohol. He couldn't sit still, so when there was no swell he would go insane. He asked the owners of the shack that we rented for permission to paint the entire place just so he would have something to do. He cleaned every crack of that place with a toothbrush, whatever it took for him to not have to sit still.

Henry was unbelievable, I never met anyone like him. He was feral. He had lived in Mentawais for years, and this guy was so broke that he owed Indonesians money, and they are some of the poorest people on earth. I thought that was wild. This guy shared a story with me that years ago he was hanging out with a girl, and they were really into each other, but at some point, she got too drunk and passed out. He decided to sleep with her anyway. He doesn't know if she remembered it or not, and it still ate at him. I just thought, *Wow, that is so dark.* I judged him for that; I didn't say anything, but I just sat there thinking how dark and fucked up that is. Something that really threw me is that a couple of years later, he ended up landing a cover of a mainstream surf magazine. It really made me wonder if karma is actually a real thing because it seems like people who do fucked-up things get rewarded all the time, but that's not for me to judge or try to figure out.

Rowan was just a typical Aussie, you know, the kind of guy who was banging prostitutes and invincible. With no shame at all, he told us a story of how he raw-dogged this Indonesian prostitute and then jumped straight on a two-week boat trip. While he was out there, gonorrhea had kicked in, and he had no way to get in for treatment. It was just pure hell and pain. To this day I am still in tears laughing over the way he told this story.

~ ~ ~

It wasn't all sharing stories of a dark past. Probably two weeks into the trip, Darren and I did a town mission to pick up some supplies. I was feeling a bit down at the time. These trips are incredible but they are also really challenging, especially when there are no waves. There's really not a whole lot else to do other than sharing stories around the group. It was painfully hot, and the food we were eating made it so we had really low energy. It was nice to go into town and get a break from the jungle. It was still a Third World country, but at least going to town gave you a sliver of normalcy.

Just as we arrived in town, a massive rainstorm hit. We were like a couple of wet rats and were trying to find a place to duck into for shelter. We spotted a sign that said *bakery* and headed inside. We couldn't believe what we discovered.

It was the most delicious bakery, almost like finding an oasis in the desert. We definitely didn't expect to find anything like that in this part of the world. We were so excited to be out of the rain and were trying everything that looked good, which meant we were eating everything. Darren and I were chatting with the bakery staff when someone came from the back. He looked different from the local African-looking people; he looked Indonesian. He opened his mouth, and he spoke English, which was rare in this area. We learned that he was originally from Bali, living in Papua where he opened this bakery.

He saw that Darren and I were completely drenched, our soaking wet clothes dripping on the bakery floor. He invited us to the back of the bakery where he had a lounge-like area. He made us tea and gave us dry shirts to wear. They were really exotic-looking T-shirts with flowers and intricately printed designs. By no means were these shirts Darren or I would usually wear, but we were so grateful for this man's kindness. As beat up as the shirt is, I still have it to this day.

From that point on, we made it a mission to go to the bakery as often as we could.

It wasn't all sweet treats. One of the guys ended up getting malaria. While I was able to dodge the malaria, I did end up with a pretty severe staph infection. I got a cut on my leg from the motorbike. It was just a small accident that ended up turning into a really bad staph infection. The whole bottom of my leg swelled up. I couldn't even walk; it was like a balloon. With no doctors or anything out there, I was able to find this little shithole clinic where they gave me amoxicillin. That amoxicillin saved my life. I had Darren telling me, "Shit, dude,

I think they're gonna have to amputate," the whole time. He was just fucking with me, but I was so scared. The amoxicillin kicked in, and the swelling went down to the point where I was able to fly back to Bali.

There's something about the trips that are focused on discovery that excite me the most. I felt it years earlier in Newfoundland. Out in Papua, we didn't see one other surfer the entire time. What that showed me was that there's still so much to see out there. People act like the whole world has been discovered, but there's so much that hasn't been touched.

[WEST AUSTRALIA —JANUARY 2012]

Back in Indonesia, still buzzing from our time in Papua, Darren and I were trying to figure out how we were going to accomplish our dreams of staying on the road and not going back home to California, with no backing.

We met an Australian guy who worked in the mines in West Oz. We had already heard about how much money you can make there in a short period of time, so we were interested. Darren and I were still under thirty, which meant that we could easily get one-year working visas allowing us to go down to Australia and work legally. We decided that's exactly what we would do, and so we flew from Bali to Perth. There we posted up with a guy I knew from Brisbane for a couple of days.

We bought a 1991 Ford Falcon wagon, blue, equipped with a kangaroo bar on the front. They call it a roobar for hitting kangaroos in Australia cause there are so many out there. And we did. Darren ended up hitting and killing a massive kangaroo with our car that sort of dented—well, more like totaled—the front right end in. It was still drivable, but it was not pretty. We made our way down toward Margaret River, which was, and still is, an iconic surfing destination. Yet again, it was a dream of mine to go there, and honestly, I never thought I'd be lucky enough to make it. When I say iconic, some of the most amazing surfing cinematography comes out of Western Australia because the water is crystal clear, and the waves are massive and possess such raw power. As a surfer, you immediately know when you see footage of West Oz.

When we got down there, we reached out to a friend of a friend who made some introductions and pointed us in the right direction. I'm telling you, in the surf world, everybody is connected one way or another. It was no big deal to call someone up and let them know you were in town, looking for a place to stay or work in order to continue the search for waves. So there we were, meeting up with this guy Owen who was originally from my hometown but hadn't been back in thirty years or so. At this point, he was basically an Australian. Years ago, he had bought a property overlooking a well-known wave called Yallingup. There were plenty of limestone caves in the area, and Owen happened to have one on his property. His place became a world-famous surfing destination house. Musicians recorded albums there, and they used to have massive techno parties. All the parties stopped when someone apparently died from a meth overdose. The way the story goes, he had a heart attack while at a party there and that was it. All the parties stopped happening, and everything shut down.

In a pretty ingenious shift, Owen decided to use the property to host weddings. The property had a natural cave amphitheater in the backyard. It was so crazy to see a cave there just behind the house. It was beautiful. So when we arrived, they were using the property to host weddings. People would book the house and the amphitheater.

There was a trailer in the back that was completely thrashed. Once Owen learned we were from his hometown, he welcomed us with open arms, letting us live in the trailer in the backyard. He got us both jobs working in construction, which was perfect cause we were almost flat broke at this point. There we were, Darren and I camping out in the bush behind this beautiful property, waking up at 5:00 a.m. every day to go work construction. The water in the showers came out brown, but we learned it was actually from natural tea tree oil, which made you feel fresh and amazing (at least that's what Owen told us).

We were so grateful for the setup. The work was pure hell under the harsh Australian sun, but we had a place to stay, had some money coming in, and we were surfing in West Australia every day.

"How long you fellas going to be here?" Owen asked.

"Ah, well, we'll work for you as long as you need."

"Well, I want you to build 'em all." Which meant years of work if we wanted it.

Owen was building prefab homes for a housing community in addition to a vineyard with some locals. Come to find out the locals referred to him as "Owen the Scammer" because he was always scheming and trying to rip people off. You can only do that shit for so long before people see what you're doing. We knew it wouldn't be a forever gig, but what an experience.

We were down in West Oz for close to five months. We were really isolated. Overall, Western Australia is a really lonely place. It was just Darren and I. We got along well, but being together nonstop in this remote place definitely had an impact on us. We were butting heads and had a couple of blowups.

Around the same time, my good friend Cole reached out to me saying he wanted to come out from California. He wanted to meet up in Bali, which was perfect cause it gave Darren and I some space after living together in that trailer for so long. I flew back to Bali to meet up with him, and we did some surf trips around Indo before flying back to West Oz together. He applied for and got a working visa. Cole was the cousin of one of the greatest surfers in the world. He grew up surfing with the best and was an amazing surfer himself. I really looked up to that family. It felt so crazy to me that he would want to get on my program of traveling the world and working on the road. Cole did really well with surfing; he had sponsorships when he was younger and could have gone really far, but at a certain point, it all fell apart for him. He decided to bail on the surf industry and go to college and get his degree, which I respect him for. From my perspective, it felt like he had a lot of resentment toward the surf industry and maybe a bit of shame or guilt that his cousin was so successful in his career. Living in someone else's shadows isn't fun. I've felt that with my own cousin's success in surfing.

Visas in hand, we headed to West Oz and met up with Darren. We spent a month there and were planning to pick up work in construction with Owen. As luck would have it, something fell through with Owen's project. Darren ended up getting laid off and Cole learned that his dad was going through a pretty serious surgery, and his mom needed him to get back home to help out. That was it for this leg. Even though we had an incredible time together surfing heavy waves, it was time for us to wrap our stay.

~ ~ ~

Cole flew home, and Darren flew back to Indonesia to be with his girlfriend. As for me, I decided I would stay in Australia a bit longer. I flew solo to the East Coast of Australia to connect with some of my childhood friends. They were a group of Aussies that would come over and hang out with my crew in San Diego. There was cheap cocaine and booze in California, so they would go huge, and girls loved them. Then my crew would go over to Australia and mirror them. Even though I was sober at this point, I was still in touch with everyone, so I flew out to North Stradbroke Island off the Coast of Brisbane.

I posted up with this kid Tory and I started laying tile with their buddy named Crickey. This guy, Coke Can Crickey, was an ugly bloke, but the whole island knew he had a bat like a Coke can, massive and thick. He set the bar on the island, so even though he wasn't the best-looking guy, he had women coming at him to get a piece of the Coke can. He would always say, "Yeah, mate, they always wonder what they got themselves into." Aussies are some of the funniest and raunchiest people you'll ever meet. You can really see how it was a criminal state that became a country; you see it in the culture in a really funny way. Their slang is second to none.

Laying tile was brutal, way more intense than I ever expected. Crickey had already undergone three major back surgeries as a result of nonstop tile work and he was only twenty-seven. People don't realize it but it completely thrashes your back. Within the first month, I already felt my back going out. I'm not sure if it would have helped, but at this time I would never stretch, I just powered through surfing and laying tile. I started to feel my back going out and got nervous, especially because of what happened to my dad when he threw his back out, leading to a relapse.

Darren and I never ended up landing jobs in the West Oz mines, but I kept feelers out there. It was definitely harder to get the work than either of us had imagined. I kept pushing, checking in with some contacts until finally, something opened up. There's a sand mine on North Stradbroke Island where my friend Ezra happened to be working as a bulldozer operator in the dry mining unit. He put in a good word for me so when one of their employees bowed out and quit suddenly, they threw me in the operator seat. I had zero experience operating heavy equipment, but they were in a jam and needed someone, and I was eager and willing. These things are way harder to operate than you'd think. First of all, they are massive, D10 bulldozers. You can't just hop in and start cutting clean lines. It takes months of fierce attention to get the blade to cut a clean line in the sand. I was horrible at the beginning, but I began to pick it up.

I got the job, and I worked my ass off. I was working twelve-hour shifts. I would go for four days in a row and then switch to four nights in a row. I had no idea what time it was, let alone what day. You're going for twelve hours in this bulldozer, just going all night, getting rattled around this cage. You have to go nonstop, cutting and pushing the sand into the dry mining unit. Even though it was rough, there were parts of the job that were fun. It's a really good job to have with ADD because there's nonstop action. I was making the most money I've ever made, which wasn't crazy amounts, but it was $1,200 cash a week and I was working toward my goal of saving $20,000 to allow me to get my own place back in Bali. I had never had a place of my own, so this was something I was really excited about and was determined to make happen.

We were mining things like zircon, ilmenite, and other things that I was told they use to make TVs and cell phones. In short, there was massive money in it. The owner of the mine was a billionaire. I got to meet him, and a side note on how billionaires shake your hand: I've only ever met two of them, but from what I have experienced they always grab the end of your hand, more at the fingers than the hand. It's like they can't bring themselves to give you a proper handshake. Come to find out it's a superiority thing, like you're not on their level. For some reason, this has always triggered me. In my eyes, no one is better than anyone else. The way I see it, no matter how much money you have, no matter how good you are in your sport or industry, you should show the same level of respect to everyone you meet.

Working with my buddy Ezra was a trip. He was about my height, fair-skinned with completely tatted sleeves. He was a top junior surfer when he was young. He and his best friend grew up competing together; while Ezra found himself working in the mines, his friend made the highest stage, the World Tour. There was definitely a bit of jealousy there, but he was perfectly suited for the mines. His voice was gritty, almost like gravel, and he had the mouth of a sailor.

I was operating the bulldozer when he came on the radio. "You there, Mike?" he said in a thick Australian accent.

"Yeah, I'm here."

"Hey, you Seppo cunt, stop pushing dirt over the dry mining unit."

"Listen, if you keep talking shit, I'm gonna come down there and smash your fat, ugly, Aussie head into the wall."

"You reckon you could?" he said, exaggerating the "could" in a long, drawn-out Aussie sort of way.

I laughed off radio.

This type of banter was a regular thing for us. It kept us going during the seemingly endless shifts.

When you're working in the dry mining unit, it's pretty common to have to get out of the bulldozer and look down into the pit to make sure that the sand was flowing properly. This one night, I got out; I was kind of rushing through the check. I don't know why I was in a hurry; I was actually in a good mood, a good headspace. I was wearing all the appropriate dry mining gear, head-to-toe suited up, work boots, helmet, and glasses. I slipped and hit the corner of the blade of the dozer. The blade sliced through my pants and busted my kneecap open. The skin was completely open with the bone sticking out. I called my shift partner and then the manager. Following protocol meant that they had to send a boat from Brisbane out to the island to pick me up and take me to the hospital because they aren't allowed to stitch anything up on site without an X-ray in case it's fractured or there's sand in the wound. I got to the Brisbane hospital well aware that this was becoming an all-night ordeal. They took X-rays and found that everything was okay, no chipped or broken bones. They cleaned it out and stitched me up. I still have that scar on my knee today. Funny enough, it sort of looks like a smiley face.

Right around the time I gashed my knee, I reached my goal of saving $20,000. The writing was on the wall, and it was time for me to hit the road.

~ ~ ~

Let me start by saying that I love Australians. I really do, but during that time, it wasn't cool to be sober. Most Australians couldn't understand it. It wasn't something they were used to seeing or talking about openly. It felt like they were ten years behind the rest of the world.

Back in the States, it was just starting to be cool to get sober, but in Australia, it wasn't even on the radar. One night, I was at a house party with all my Aussie buddies. I was doing my usual thing of having a soda water with lime. It's not like I was hiding that I was sober, it was just easier if I didn't make a big deal out of it and blended in with some sort of refreshment. I could usually get away with this in a new place where no one knew who I was. But here on the island of North Straddie, it was a small community and everyone knew I was sober.

One of the biggest drunks on the island was at this party. You could tell that this guy was really suffering just from looking at him. He had that alcoholic look to his face, his teeth, to his body, even to his posture.

Out of nowhere from across the party, he spotted me and shouted, "Mikey, why don't you harden up and have a beer, you soft cock."

Most of the people in the house thought it was hilarious. I didn't give a shit. You have to not give a fuck about what anyone thinks of you. You have to stay sober for you. Some of my peers back home might have done otherwise just to fit in. Instead, I quickly responded with, "Maybe I would if it looked like you were having a good time." And I meant it; he looked miserable.

He didn't say a word, and there was an awkward silence at the party. I decided to leave not too long after that. It's hard to have people cut you down who don't understand that your decision to stay sober is life or death. I know that might sound dramatic, especially for people who don't have experience with addicts or addiction themselves, but if you look at my family history, it's true.

I was a little more comfortable with myself in sobriety at this point, but not that comfortable yet. Honestly, I still don't know if I'm 100 percent comfortable in a drinking or drug-taking atmosphere. I always feel a bit awkward in those situations, and I totally get it. When I was drinking and going hard, I didn't want somebody who was sober around me. I thought they were weirdos, and I couldn't understand why someone would want to be sober. There's also something about the judgment or the perceived judgment of someone sober looking down on everyone else.

In general, I sort of lost respect for Australians during my time there. It felt like everything revolved around partying no matter where you were. Every now and then someone would go out of their way to tell me that they respected what I was doing, because, for example, one of their friends died from drug- and alcohol-related issues, but it was rare. It's few and far between but some Aussies are the biggest legends you will ever meet.

[BALI, INDONESIA —MARCH 2013]

I headed back to Bali with no real plan. The way things worked out I actually flew back with Darren, who had ended up joining me in North Straddie for a bit. He worked in a restaurant making pizzas while I worked the mines.

Before going to Australia, I had met a girl from Spain. I say I had a crush on her, but it was more than that. I briefly fell in love with her, or the idea of her. Her name was Gabriela. She was gorgeous, petite, with beautifully tanned skin and long, dark, wavy hair with dark eyes to match. Looking back, I seemed to chase women who looked like and behaved like my mom. It's not uncommon for many people who had tumultuous childhoods to seek out the equal to their parents in intimate relationships.

I maintained a delusional crush on Gabriela throughout the whole year I was in Australia. I hadn't seen her, but we kept in touch, which made me believe even more that she was the one, that she was perfect, but in reality, it was something else entirely. For starters, she was a chain-smoking alcoholic, and I was sober, so that wasn't going to work out; I just didn't know it yet.

I had all this savings from working in the mines, the most money I had ever had in my life. It's not saying much, but I never had more than three grand in savings. My initial plan was to use that money to set myself up comfortably in Bali, but I was so impulsive that by the time I got to Bali, I didn't want to be there anymore; I wanted to chase this girl in Europe instead. I saw a flight on AirAsia from Bali to Paris, direct for $230, which is unheard of. That's a big flight; usually that was a $1,000 to $2,000 flight, at least. I just thought there was no way I could pass this up.

I had never been to Europe. It was a direct flight, bam, I'm going.

I got what I paid for with the flight. It was hands down the most miserable flight of my life. Completely cramped, no food, no water, horrible, fifteen hellish hours. Again, I got what I paid for. I landed in Paris right as a Siberian cold front was hitting the region. We're talking the coldest temperatures on record, and I was in board shorts and a T-shirt. I had zero clothing for cold weather, and it was so cold. I'd never experienced weather this cold; it was so cold that my esophagus was going numb. I couldn't even feel myself breathing—my fingers were going numb, too. I went straight to a store from the airport, and I bought gloves and all this warm gear. Right away, I was already spending tons of money, but I was warm and that's all I cared about.

My whole idea was to go to Spain to see Gabriela, but I hadn't made any plan beyond getting to Paris. I checked into a hotel in the heart of the city, within walking distance of the Eiffel Tower. Maybe it was the fact that it was fucking freezing or because I was by myself, but I didn't even go up the Eiffel

Tower; I just observed it from ground level. Paris, in general, was disappointing to me.

I checked in with Mark, who I had been keeping in touch with about our sobriety, and he suggested I reach out to this female surf photographer that he knew down in Portugal.

I shot her a message and she responded immediately. *Yeah, come down to Portugal, I'll pick you up, you can stay at my place. We'll surf, we'll try to get some photos. All of it.*

It was perfect. It helped me to feel like I wasn't making that big of a deal of going to Europe just for this girl that I hadn't seen for a year. But anyway, I flew down to Portugal and got to check out the coast there. What a wild and beautiful place. Talk about raw power in the ocean. It reminded me of West Australia, really spread out and dry. The people there were kind of like a European mellow version of Brazilians.

I had a great trip with the lady I stayed with, got some really fun waves, and got a chance to experience the culture. I was surprised that she made a move on me. Not an intense move or anything, she just made it clear that she was ready to go if I was. Somehow, believe it or not, I passed on it even though throughout periods of time I have walked through sex addiction, which is its own very painful, lonely, and empty road. Granted, I didn't know at the time that it was another addiction, I just thought I was being a young man. It didn't help that Jack would encourage that behavior every chance he got. So I didn't sleep with her. I knew I was going to see Gabriela soon.

I was in Portugal for two weeks when my friend Zach invited me to meet up with him in Morocco. I immediately accepted and hopped on a three-hour flight to meet up with

Zach and his buddy Tim, who happened to be a well-known surfer from California. It also just so happened that Tim was sober as well, and we spent a lot of time chatting about sobriety, AA, and the Twelve Steps. Zach wasn't AA sober but he wasn't a big drinker or drug taker. His dad committed suicide when he was young, and it sent him on this path to healing and searching and living a good, clean, healthy life. He was always positive, and it rubbed off on everyone around him. He was a pro-drop knee bodyboarder as a kid. He traveled a lot doing that and then got to a place where it wasn't fulfilling enough for him. The guys that he thought were his heroes were actually degenerates, and he wanted more so he ended up going back to school and got his degree in psychology.

I had a good time down there in Morocco with the guys, and then I flew to Madrid. I stayed with Gabriela, her sister, and her mom. The older sister was a flight attendant and the sole provider for the family. Neither the mom nor Gabriela made any money of their own. I could tell that her sister was a really good person and that she put her family first.

My time in Spain turned out to be different than I imagined, but that's life, isn't it? I'm glad I went, but also I'm glad I got to experience other places in Europe during my trip. I was too late to be with Gabriela; she had sparked things up again with her ex-boyfriend, who was living in London at the time. Looking back, it's a good thing really. One of those blessings in disguise.

She showed me her ugly side one night in a dramatic and emotional outburst. I wasn't drinking, and I wanted to keep it mellow at the house. I stayed back while Gabriela went out and drank all night. When she came home, she was screaming at everyone including me, how I didn't even come out with her that night. It was a nightmare being around a chain-smoking drunk when I was focused on my sobriety. I had to cut my losses—so I got on a plane and headed back to LA for my first trip home in a while.

[SAN DIEGO, CA —DECEMBER 2013]

After Europe, I briefly made my way back to California. After my travels, it no longer felt like home for me. There were still too many memories, too many friends who knew the old me, and still no real support. For me, California was my past; it was nothing more than a pit stop between destinations.

As I found myself in my old stomping grounds, memories came flooding back. I drove past the old dive bar where I used to get hammered. I saw the same cars and old faces in the parking lot. I continued driving, each place a milestone of pain, embarrassment, and regret. I found myself sitting in my car in front of the old container where I lived while getting sober. It was even more pathetic than I remembered. I wanted nothing more than to leave, to head back to my new life and what had become my new home, and to continue exploring.

I still had $10,000 in savings and I went ahead and bought an iPhone, a new MacBook Pro laptop, a Canon camera, and a really nice Canon lens so I could go back to Indonesia and get footage of surfing, something I never had really done before.

I can't even describe the feeling of being able to buy these things. After growing up buying Snickers bars with food stamps when they were still printed, I never imagined I would have the opportunity to travel the world, to buy myself all this stuff.

I stood there in the Apple Store thinking back on the time I lived with my dad. What would he have done if he had this kind of money? He'd go to the horse races.

I could picture it like it was yesterday. I was eleven years old. It was 1995 and we were at the Del Mar Horse Races, my dad standing in the horse paddock with his buddies.

"Alright, son, this is it. We need one more and we're into some big money."

I jumped up on the ledge to get a better look at the horse, a program curled up in my hand like a kaleidoscope.

"Hey, man, I just got a tip on Ignito; he's gonna win," Billy said, looking and sounding like Popeye.

"Fuck you, Billy. You're the kiss of death, I swear," my dad said.

"Hey, relax! I'm just telling you what I heard. This came from Davie's stable."

"Listen, Billy, you fuckin' asshole. If I win, I'm looking at about two hundred grand. I'm taking all of us to Cabo. So stop being the negative, pessimistic jinx that you've always been."

"Yeah, alright man. I won't hold my breath."

Ignoring Billy entirely, my dad shifted his focus to another one of his degenerate friends. "Hey, Lurch, whatta you got?"

Holding true to the nickname, Lurch was a beast of a human. He was about six foot five and looked just like Lurch from *The Addams Family* crossed with a big ape. He loved black women and smoking crack. Hookers called him Cochino, which means pig, because he loved eating pussy and going with no rubber. My dad used to say, "If this guy doesn't have AIDS, it doesn't exist." I know, it's insanity that I knew this as a little kid.

"Fuck, I don't know; this is a weird one, man. I put a tri together with the 1, 4, 8,1, 4, 9, boxed."

"Yeah, well if I get this home, things are looking real good, Lurch, SO COME ON YOU FUCKIN' APE!!! I'VE GOT THE HORSE NAMED LET'S GO SURFING BABY!!! WOOOHHH!!"

"Come on, Mikey, I wanna see how they look on the track," My dad said, ushering me along to the finish line.

You could feel the tension shift just before the race started. All the lowlives, grouped together, nervous, excited. I remember thinking, *What a bunch of losers.*

My dad was hands down the loudest guy in the whole track. I was mortified.

"Alright, here we go, motherfuckers!!! Let's Go Surfing!!!" Screaming and beet red, almost purple in the face.

Still embarrassed, but wanting to fit in, I took on my dad's level of excitement, slapping the program on my hand as I cheered.

"And away they go," the announcer yelled. The crowd went wild.

"WOOOHHH!!!!!" My dad screamed, his face turning more purple by the moment. I was scared that he was going to have a heart attack.

At one point my dad was running around screaming as the announcer rapid-fire called out the status of the race.

The announcer didn't miss a beat: "Let's Go Surfing has a commanding lead coming into the final stretch of the Pacific Classic. Let's Go Surfing is really pulling away from the pack now."

"Yeeaasss!!!! Let's Go Surfing, motherfucker!!!! We got it, Mikey! We got it, Mikey!" My dad screamed while pinching my ears in excitement as he ground his teeth.

"Hold on! Ignito is really making a move for it! Ignito coming on late here into these last three hundred meters."

Visibly panicked, pinching my ears as though they were now a stress ball, my dad let out a fearful, "Oh no!!!"

"Let's Go Surfing still with a strong lead; will he hold on?" the announcer asked the crowd.

"Please no! Please no!" My dad now chanting, as if it were a mantra, while he ran toward the finish line.

"Ignito moving very fast from the outside. This is gonna be a close one! Here they come, head for head at the wire!!!"

After the longest minute of our lives, he came back on. "Wow, ladies and gentlemen, that was a close one. We have a photo finish."

My dad was flipping out, his face now a deep shade of purple. "Did he get it? Did he get it?"

Billy bravely chimed in, "I don't know. I don't know."

After a long and tense silence, Lurch threw in, "It was close, man."

The announcer came back on. "After a very tight photo finish and a long wait, we have a winner. Ignito!"

Furious and completely defeated, my dad screamed, "Ohhh nooo!!!! Fuck!! Every fuckin' time!!!"

I watched from a distance, not sure what to say. I felt heartbroken and sad for my dad, but I couldn't understand why we were here betting money on horses when we were living in his mattress store like roaches.

We left the track and boarded a double-decker bus. Neither of us spoke. When we finally arrived at the store, my dad looked at me and said, "Mikey, we got close, son. I'm sorry, son. I was hoping we would be able to get a house. I'm miserable."

I had no more solace to offer him. "Alright, Dad, I'm going to sleep," I said as I grabbed my sleeping bag and went to find a plastic-covered mattress to sleep on.

Memories like these were flooding my mind the entire time I was back in San Diego. It's really hard to be back in an unsupportive, toxic environment when you are so dedicated to sobriety. I got what I came there for, bought my new gear, and headed out.

[BALI, INDONESIA —DECEMBER 2013]

By the time I got back to Bali, I was broke. Not close to broke—I had no money. There had been some fraud on my account, and someone had stolen the last $700 from my Indonesia account. I had zero dollars and was staying at Jack's house when I got a call from this Englishman, William, who I met in an AA meeting in Bali.

I always went to AA meetings in other countries. It was usually one of the first things I did when I got off the plane in a new place. I quickly found out that you could travel the world and stay sober. Not only that, but you have the opportunity to meet people from all over the world and have the connection of sobriety instantly. It has truly been a gift. I've gotten jobs, had people invite me to stay at their places in different parts of the world, and have even met some of my best friends in meetings.

William was just checking in on me, talking about sobriety, and I let him know where I was at. Right away he said, "You know, I am completely swamped, beyond buried, and I need a worker. Do you want to work for me? You can start working right away."

It was perfect timing. I said, "Of course, yes." I never really had time to think about whether or not I wanted to do something, it was always pure survival, sink or swim. It's been like this since day one, which felt like a curse, but in many ways, it's been a blessing because it's forced me to do so many things I never would have done without having that life path.

The next day I started working. William put me on a small salary cap and started training me right away. Here I was working in a Third World country where you could get a full meal for $1, finding ways to provide provisions to super yachts that were sometimes fifty to one hundred million dollars, visiting Indonesia. It was wild to see these super yachts in a place where everybody was poor. When I say poor, I mean that everyone was living in poverty, wearing the same clothes every day, struggling to make ends meet, but there were no actual homeless people. Everyone lived in a community of shacks and took care of each other. This struck me in comparison to America, which is such a wealthy country. In the States, you see homeless people far too often living on the streets, completely alone with no community. It's actually infuriating that, for such a wealthy country, we still have homelessness when somehow a place like Bali doesn't. That doesn't mean Bali has it all figured out. One thing that struck me and was in stark contrast to the lavish yachts was the lack of cleanliness in Bali. You think you're pulling up to paradise, but in reality, there's a foot-high pile of trash on the beach that extends for miles.

Getting on these boats in the harbor, I discovered a whole other world that I never knew existed. Many of the people who own these yachts have their own submarine, helicopter, and gym on board. It's like a multistory luxury apartment on the water. The thing I can't get over is that the owners are rarely even on the yachts. The crew would always tell me how the owners spent maybe two weeks a year onboard. The crew are the ones living on the ship. They travel the world to meet the owners, our clients, anywhere they want them to be. They literally do laps around the globe in these super yachts.

Having had the opportunity to meet and spend time with the captains and the crew, I quickly learned that I never wanted to be in their shoes. They lived for their employers. They were constantly overworked with all the responsibilities of keeping a boat like that running. Between endless polishing, engineering work, and moving the boat around the world, they had little to no time for themselves. Sure, they were seeing the world, but it felt like they were trapped.

I was learning a lot, but at a certain point working in Indonesia wears you down in a way that's hard to explain. Anyone who has worked there or in other Third World countries as an expat understands. Every day you're battling language barriers, corruption and lies, backstabbing, and the red tape that comes with it. When the government officials see these super yachts coming in, their eyes light up, and they see dollar signs. We somehow end up having to be the middlemen between the government officials and our clients who own the super yachts. In addition to the corruption, it was so hard even just getting around the city. You're dealing with crazy Third World traffic where there are absolutely no rules and excessive exhaust and pollution, which nobody expects when they come to Bali.

Imagine you're trying to get somewhere in the center of the city to get a spare part for the engineer whose yacht is departing that evening, all while it's boiling hot and 100 percent humidity, and you're riding a motorbike.

All of this, every day, took its toll on me. I was struggling. I've battled depression my whole life, most of the time completely unaware that that's what it was. I was in a down period as was William, my boss. I don't know if we weren't connecting with people or just weren't feeling fulfilled, but we were both in a slump. It always seems like when you're in these down periods, God will send you a gift; he will remind you of your purpose.

We received a call from one of the captains who had just docked. One of his crew members was in a bad way. She drank the whole bar, broke a bunch of stuff, and created a really big problem on the boat. The captain asked that we pick her up and take her to the airport. Before dropping her off, William and I spent time talking to her about being alcoholics and being sober ourselves. We let her know that there's help and walked her through what the Twelve Step program was. We didn't go out of our way in search of someone to help; it fell into our laps. We were able to share the gift of sobriety with someone who was struggling, which has happened many times over the years. When you need it the most, God will give you that wake-up call that puts you in a situation that gives you perspective. For William and me, it really pulled us up out of our depression. I was able to look at my situation and say, *Okay, Mike, you have quality problems today. If you weren't sober, you wouldn't even be having these issues cause you'd be stuck in a gutter somewhere.*

I worked with William at the super yacht agency for some time, and even though I was grateful for the opportunity, I came to the conclusion that this wasn't the job for me. I gave my notice and headed back to Australia to do my taxes.

[TEAHUPO'O, TAHITI —MARCH 2014]

I wasn't sure how taxes in Australia worked. I knew I had to file from working in the mines but I wasn't sure if I was going to owe money or get it back. Luck was on my side and I found out that I was going to get a check for $7,000 coming back to me. I knew I was going to take that money and go to Tahiti because I wanted to surf Teahupo'o (a world-famous wave) before I died, and I didn't know if I'd have the money to do it later.

I flew through Auckland, New Zealand, laying over for a night. I cruised around the city, and while it's exciting, it can also be lonely when you're traveling by yourself. It was beautiful, and although I love traveling solo, there are times when it's not as fun when you don't have someone to share it with.

My friend Evan flew out from San Diego to meet me two weeks into the trip. I had surfed my brains out almost every day. It was a long paddle out to the break, close to twenty minutes. It was really far, and the waves were more powerful than anything I had ever experienced. One afternoon, after we had already surfed in the morning, Evan turned to me and said, “Hey, I’m going to paddle back out.” He was still full of energy because he had just gotten there.

“Nah, I’m not going. I’m too…my arms are dead. I’m tapped.”

“Fucking please, let’s go, let’s go, let’s go,” he kept saying.

Somehow he talked me into it and I paddled back out with him. When we got out there, it was looking kind of shitty, or average—I mean, it’s never really shitty there—Teahupo’o is basically heaven on earth, but the waves weren’t optimal.

Somewhere between thirty minutes to an hour into the session, everything changed. The wind went completely glassy, the waves picked up, and we started getting wave after wave of pure fun. Before we knew it, overhead sets were rolling in. It was just Evan and I out there and this one local Tahitian boy. This kid was really talented and has since gone on to become one of the biggest chargers from Tahiti.

Evan and I were sitting out the back of the peak. I saw this west bowl coming in, and I was sitting inside of Evan so I was in position. I put my head down and started booking it toward the channel. It looked like I was too deep, but I just put it in my mind that I was going to make this wave, and that’s usually the mindset that I have. That mindset has gotten me into some trouble. I’ve broken a lot of boards over the years. I’ve had people tell me that I break more boards than anyone they’ve ever met, and it isn’t a compliment. I get into this mindset where I tell myself I’m going to make it. If I tell myself I can do something, there’s no room for failure. In my mind, I’ve already made it. And even though I don’t make it most of the time, or maybe even a lot of the time, the times I have made it have been the most incredible rides of my life.

This one wave was symbolic of that.

I put my head down and I paddled as hard as I could. I felt like I was too deep, but in my mind, there was no not making it. I got under the ledge, airdropped, hooked under the lip, and I saw the wave completely go past me like a freight train. I was deep in the barrel. I did three of the biggest pumps that I could possibly do to gain speed. I remember being so deep in the barrel and the spit completely blowing past me, engulfing me. It was blowing past me to the point where I couldn't see anything and I was behind the foam ball.

Being in the barrel in this moment felt like I was reading braille. I know that might sound corny but that's what it felt like. I couldn't see anything, and I was waiting for the lip of the wave to detonate on my head but I just stayed in it. Eventually, the spit cleared. I was still deep in the barrel and then came flying out.

The local Tahitian boy was paddling out, screaming at the top of his lungs. As I pulled out of the wave and into the channel, I was also screaming, almost going into convulsions cause I had never experienced adrenaline like that. He paddled over to me and hugged me, the two of us going back and forth just saying, "Oh my God! Ahhh! Oh my God!"

I'll never forget that moment. To this day it's still one of the most amazing experiences I've had in surfing. Not only in surfing, but in my life.

[SOLANA BEACH, CA —APRIL 2014]

I left Tahiti and flew back to California. I had just wrapped a full lap around the globe, working and traveling. I had seen so many incredible things, met wonderful people, and yet somehow, back in my hometown, it was as though nothing had changed.

My parents were still struggling.

Still using.

Still homeless.

"Don't you guys think it's time for a change?" I asked. "You've been doing this for long enough. I can't stand to see you live like this. It really hurts."

My parents just stared off into space—it was like I was speaking another language.

"Save the preaching kid," my dad finally said. "Live and let live."

I was annoyed to hear that they had pretty much given up on life, but still, they were my parents and I wanted to help.

"How about I help you guys sell this car and we get you a van? I'll cover the difference."

"Yeah, anything would be better than this. You think we can afford it?" my dad asked as my mom was still pilled out.

"Yeah, I saved some money working in Australia. We can sell this and I can cover the rest. Let's find something."

It just so happened that this lady I knew was selling her old Dodge Campervan. It would allow them more space. It was bright orange (later to be known around town as "Orange Crush"). It had a double-size bed and a little stove and sink inside.

"How much you want for it?" I asked the lady.

"Ohhh, fifteen hundred should do it."

"Okay, perfect. You've got a deal."

We were able to clean up their Hyundai and sell it for exactly $1,500, and my parents moved straight into the van.

~ ~ ~

I didn't see many friends when I was in town but I did meet up to surf with an old buddy, Terry. He was older than me, in his fifties but at heart he was still eighteen. He rocked the backward hat and had tons of tattoos.

"Yeah, Mike, how's traveling been? How was Indo?" Terry asked as we paddled out past the break.

It felt so weird to be paddling out at my home break after so much time away. All those years here surfing drunk or hungover. It was refreshing to just be out there sober, having a chill session with an old friend.

"From the first trip out there it's just been insane every time. I'm telling you the boat trip I took was unreal; we got the sickest waves from Sumba all the way to Timor. We didn't see one other boat the whole time," I said, drifting off, daydreaming about being back there. "I've done a lot of trips over the past couple of years, and something just keeps bringing me back to Indo."

"No way! I can't wait to go explore that place at some point. You're lucky, young buck."

I proceeded to tell Terry about my adventures, but something pulled me back to that first trip, that dreamlike surfing boat trip. I told Terry how we went from island to island surfing perfect waves with no one around. It was just me and a crew of seven guys. Seven guys who smoked joints and drank beers daily while I didn't.

"So," Terry asked, "what's the plan now?"

"I don't know; I feel so torn. I want to help my parents, but they don't want to help themselves. I really can't stay here," I said as I looked off at the vast, open ocean. "One of the guys I met on that boat trip recently offered me a job out there. He owns a series of surf shops in Southeast Asia. The job is mine if I want it."

"It sounds like life is pulling you back out there; just go with it!"

Smiling into the sunset, I knew he was right.

[BINGIN BEACH, INDONESIA —JULY 2014]

It felt good to be back in Bali, but that feeling shifted almost immediately. The guy who had offered me the job completely flaked. I was at a loss; all my money had gone into getting back to Bali, and here I was without a job when I arrived. I was beyond defeated.

Luckily, I had a close friend from home living in the area, and he happened to be sober as well. It was amazing to have good people in pockets of the world, and it was somewhat funny that so many of them happened to be from back home. There was something unique and special about it, like keeping the best parts of home and leaving the baggage.

Christian was great. He was a ladies' man and a partier when he was younger but now lived a clean, spiritual life. He is super committed to his wife, Jessica, and his kids, which is something I really admire about him. He's got a healthy amount of ego that can lead one to think he's pretentious, but he's not. He greatly enjoys being of service.

Looking at my glum face, he asked, "So what's going on, Mikey?"

"I don't know, man," I said, shaking my head. "I came back out to Indo for a job that fell through. I'm in a slump. I've been sober for five years and have nothing to show for it."

Sobriety had allowed me to do a lap around the globe, make more money than I ever had, and here I was saying I had nothing to show for being sober. This is a perfect example of how addicts are way too hard on themselves.

"Well, I don't like seeing you struggling. I'm slammed here at the restaurant and I'm tired of dealing with people. Why don't you come help me here?" Christian asked, genuinely offering out of kindness.

I hated the idea of being a charity case or having someone tell me that I was struggling, but to be fair I was, and I was smart enough to know I needed the opportunity.

"Yeah, I'd be open to that if you need the help."

"Great, you can start tomorrow if you want!!" Christian said, laughing.

Honestly, it was great for me. I started to get into a really good flow between surfing and working. I spent a lot of time with Christian and Jessica. It was the first time I spent time around a healthy couple, and it felt good to have such a strong, positive influence around me. I even started to get some exposure in surfing again because I was surfing consistently and living more healthily than I had in a long time. *Surfline*, a global surfing forecast website, ran a shot of me in their Indonesia feature, and even *BaliBelly* magazine gave me some push on their socials.

Even though I was doing well, I wasn't aware of the subtle addictions that were starting to surface for me during this period. I was desperately looking for ways to comfort myself.

I know now that it's because I never felt safe in this world, but at the time I was just trying to quiet the noise in my head, to survive the turmoil. I lost myself in food, coffee, sugar, and sex.

One night, after I temporarily found comfort in sex with a stranger, I started to think that I was acting like my father. Sure, I might be sober, but I was still looking at women, at sex, the way he did, as if they were toys.

Back when I was eleven, not long after the horse races, my dad took me to Mexico with his buddy Dylan. It wasn't the first time, or the last, but my dad had arranged for a prostitute at the hotel.

"Alright, I'll see you guys a little later," my dad said, smirking as though he was about to successfully lure her in, not that he was paying for her.

"Ahhh, come on, Dad! Let me get some!" I said, trying to be cool but having no idea what I was asking.

"Yeah, come on, Nicholas, he's ready. Let the kid get a little," Dylan said in a gluttonous way, always in support of any and all bad decisions.

An hour later, I was sitting on the hotel bed watching TV when my dad strolled in with a bit of guilt and shame behind him. He stepped to the side and let the lady into the room first, as a gentleman should. I don't know what I expected, but it wasn't that. She was in her late thirties, curly wavy hair, smiling way too much, making her caked-on makeup crease. She was wearing a short, tight skirt and an even tighter tank top that showed her large fake tits. Uncomfortable, I looked down and saw her high heels. I remember they were too small for her feet and too high for her to walk normally in.

Always liking to wash up before the act, my dad said,

"Alright, son, here you go," as he entered the bathroom to hop in the shower, but not before he turned back to say, "You take care of him, alright?" as though this was totally normal.

"Hola," she said through her teeth, still smiling.

I smiled nervously, my awkward eleven-year-old embarrassment clearly showing.

She sat next to me on the bed, aware of my age but clearly trying to ignore it. "Poppa es local, si?"

Nervousness spilling over, "Ahhh, I have to go. Dad! I'm gonna be with Dylan!" I said as I sprinted out of the room before jumping into the passenger seat of Dylan's car.

"What happened, Mikey?" he said, smiling ear to ear.

"Uhhh, Dad's up there with that broad," I said, mimicking the way my dad described women.

"Did you get some?"

"Naw, she was rough."

Laughing like a joker, "alright, you can come with me." Dylan said as he passed me a joint.

I grabbed the joint and took a puff.

Looking back now, I despised the way my dad behaved but somehow, someway, I ended up repeating his behaviors in my own way. I wasn't paying for prostitutes but I was treating sex as transactional.

~ ~ ~

The more time I spent with genuinely good people like Christian and Jessica, the more I realized I had grown up surrounded by depravity and negativity. My dad always had these weird characters around that he considered his friends, which is wild to think about because the way he treated them was horrible. I began to see that it wasn't funny the way I thought it was when I was younger; it was just cruel.

My dad had this friend, he was a strange little homeless dude who hung out at the mattress store on a regular basis. He was a mechanic and my dad constantly had him wrenching on our old cars. He was schizophrenic and delusional, always having conversations with himself out loud. He looked and smelled filthy and seemed to smoke about three packs a day, saying that the smoking helped his hay fever. He also had a hernia that he couldn't afford to fix, so he was constantly rubbing himself around the balls.

My dad was the ultimate belittler. The guy's real name was Mick, but my dad had the pleasure of renaming him Leprechaun. We were so mean to this poor guy (my dad, me, Mark); we were awful. Looking back, I'm ashamed of how I treated him, but that's exactly how my dad raised me to be. We would do things like throw a Nerf football and tag him in the head from behind while he was working on a car. He would usually erupt, screaming things like, "OH WELL FUCK!!!!"

This one time, Leprechaun and my dad were butting heads, apparently over the price that my dad paid him for a job. According to my dad, everything was okay and he was paid in full, but that's not how Leprechaun saw it. One day he showed up in the front of the mattress store, screaming, "PAY ME, YOU CHEAP MOTHERFUCKER, PAY ME, PAY ME!!"

It turned into this massive scene, with all the people from the surrounding shops coming out to see my dad chasing Leprechaun down the street like he was going to kill him. That little fucker moved quick, got in his car, and peeled out of there.

The ironic part is that after all the years of my dad giving Leprechaun shit and belittling him, my dad ended up homeless, living in his car—at times, parked next to Leprechaun.

[BINGIN BEACH, INDONESIA —SEPTEMBER 2014]

I was hanging out at the café when I met her.

Kendra was a twenty-five-year-old Australian-Kiwi mix. Petite with a lean frame and an incredible body. She had blonde curly hair. She was beautiful. Despite all this, I remember that I wasn't drawn to her in a sexual way. It didn't matter anyways because she had a boyfriend.

"Hey, you guys wanna go surf Nyang Nyang?" I asked. "It's probably picking up a lot more swell."

"Sure, I'm down," Kendra said eagerly before checking with her friends who ultimately ended up joining.

After the surf, the crew headed back to the café. Jessica greeted us as we entered. She was a true southern girl at heart, a North Carolina native who found her way to Christian and to Bali. She had a kindness and a wisdom about her, but she was also quick to judge and loved to gossip. "Nobodie's poifect," as my dad always said.

"How was it?" She asked with a little smirk that told me she knew it was big.

"Ahhh, I think everyone was a bit over their head. It was big," I said.

"Really?" Jessica asked as Kendra couldn't help but jump in.

"You were in over your head too," Kendra said with a tone that bordered between bitchy and embarrassed. She let out a fake, high-pitched laugh. I would later learn she does this whenever she is uncomfortable, which seemed to happen often for someone with her ego.

"Yeah, I know," I said, knowing full well I was absolutely fine, but not in the mood to get into it with her. My first impression of her was that she was a bitch.

[BINGIN, INDONESIA —NOVEMBER 2014]

I was in a really good space. Things at the café were continuing to go well, and I was learning a lot from Christian and Jessica. They were such genuine and honest people with a lot of integrity and strong morals; they still are. Being around that was good for me. I needed it.

I had been working at and managing the café for close to six months when undercover immigration officers strolled in. I didn't take note of them at first; my head was down and I was doing some work on the computer.

"Hello, sir, are you Mr. Mike?" the man asked.

Looking up, smiling, I took in his tourist attire. Buttoned-up Hawaiian shirt, lightweight shorts, flip-flops, and a camera around his neck.

"Yeah, that's me."

I saw his lips curl into a conniving smile, clearly thinking to himself, *Gotcha.* As he pulled out his badge, I quickly eyed the word "Immigrasi."

"Can you come with me, sir? I am immigration officer

and you do not have working visa. We take you into Kuta for questioning."

Completely caught off guard, I froze internally. On the outside, I played it as cool as possible as I muttered, "Okay, sir, I'll come with you guys, no problem."

As I stood up to follow him out, I realized that another guy was in the process of pulling in Christian as well.

I went into complete shock. You hear so many horror stories in Indonesia of people who get completely screwed over by immigration and the police. In Indonesia, and many other Third World countries, they can basically do anything they want. It's all about money and extortion. People in Bali who are caught with drugs are sentenced to life in prison, or they are executed. I've heard of it happening plenty of times, and enough books like *Hotel K* back that up.

I did my best to stay calm as they brought me into an interrogation room. The first time around I have no idea how long I was in there. Time seemed to have stopped, or sped up, I'm really not sure. They kept rapid-fire questioning me, trying to get me to say on the record that I was working without a visa. Every time they asked, I said I wasn't. I don't know if this is standard protocol—honestly, who knows if there even is a standard protocol—but they told me to go home and come back the next day and that I was in big trouble.

Every day for a month, I went back and forth from my home to the interrogation room at the immigration office. It was the same questions on repeat and the same attitude, like they were toying with me.

"If you guilty, you go to jail," they would say.

Christian was in the same position. He hired a local

Indonesian woman to represent the restaurant, which luckily included me as well. The lady negotiated on our behalf and was able to secure a deal. The terms were that we each had to pay $3,500 USD and would be deported from the country for twenty-four hours, but could return with the promise that we wouldn't work again. If we couldn't pay, we would go straight to jail.

Christian took the money out of the restaurant and covered the fee for both of us, and just like that, we were deported to Singapore. I was in the clear, but I was out of a job again.

I had the all-too-familiar feeling that it seems like I'm not allowed to experience success in this life. I'll be in a good place, experiencing some stability, and then suddenly I'm back in fight-or-flight.

[MENTAWAIS, INDONESIA —JANUARY 2015]

I hadn't left Bali since my run-in with immigration. It had been some time, and while I was a bit nervous about traveling after everything, I was jonesing to get a trip in. My buddy Zane called me up and told me he was managing a new premier, luxury land resort in the Mentawais. They had a medic bow out of an upcoming trip and they had nobody to step in. Zane was from my hometown, and we had spent time together in Bali over the past few years. He was ten years older than me and was one of the best surfers to come out of my hometown during the '90s and 2000s. He knew I had grown up surfing and he also knew I had a background as a first responder being an ocean lifeguard for six years in San Diego. Zane told me the situation and invited me out for a two-week stay on the island. All I had to do was pay for my $100 flight from Bali to the Mentawais and the rest was taken care of.

The Mentawais in Indonesia is considered to have the most perfect surf in the world. It used to be that only the top pros could go to this location because their sponsors could afford to send them on expensive boat trips. There were no land camps up until this point. Because it is so expensive to stay at Kandui, it is yet another place that I thought I would never get to experience.

I couldn't believe my luck with that call. Within two days I was heading from Bali to the Disney World of surfing. Getting there wasn't easy; I had to take two flights and a four-hour boat ride to get to the island. I never get seasick, and I expected the channel to be flat, so I ate a big meal before getting on the boat from Padang to Kandui. I have never been so sick in my life. The waves were big and the channel was beyond rough. That four-hour ride on a small boat turned into seven hours of treachery. I spent five of those hours vomiting, just praying for the boat ride to finish. By the end, I had nothing left to vomit, just bile. I was lying on the floor of the boat, curled in a ball, praying. I'd look over and see a handful of other people going through the same thing.

"Holy shit! You are green, dude," Zane said as he saw me emerging from the boat, thankful to be on land.

It took me some time to find my footing. I drank some fluids and ate some papaya to try and settle my stomach before falling straight asleep.

The next day I was up at 4:00 a.m. As a surf guide, you have to wake up super early to figure out the conditions for the day and to determine where you're going to take the clients surfing. This place was incredible. You have all these small islands within a short distance of each other. You have wind and swell wrapping around the islands coming from every direction, meaning that there's always somewhere firing when there's swell.

Even though the swell wasn't a ten out of ten, I got some

incredible waves at places like Kandui Lefts, Hideaways, and many others. After ten days of getting up at 4:00 a.m., and going all day in the sun and waves, I was exhausted. During one session, I pulled into a barrel and the foam ball bucked me off my board. I dove off the board into the turbulent waters, getting ragdolled but doing my best to protect myself from the shallow reef. Out of nowhere, I feel this CRACK to my cheekbone. Even though my eyes were closed and it was dark underwater, everything went completely white. It was almost like I forgot I was underwater and that I was even surfing. I don't know how much time had passed, but luckily I came to and made it back to the surface. After getting back to the boat, I looked at my board and saw that the rail of my surfboard had been caved in about six inches. Imagine someone asking you to hold still while they use a surfboard like a baseball bat to your head; that's what it felt like.

I had all the symptoms of a concussion: nausea, confusion, blurred vision, and trouble focusing. I made the smart call to rest on the boat for the remainder of the session.

However, on the way back to camp, we stopped to check Hideaways, and of course, it was the best I had seen it so far on my trip. It's a perfect barreling left and there was no way I wasn't going to paddle out. I didn't know if I would ever get back to the Mentawais, so this was probably my last chance.

I caught a few good waves to warm up and then waited it out the back to get the wave I was looking for. All of the guests knew what had happened to me in the previous session and they kept asking if I was okay. After all, I was filling in for what would have been their medic, and I was the one who got a concussion and then paddled back out. Before jumping out of the boat, I made sure everyone knew I was all right. While I was sitting out the back, one of the best waves that I had seen came in. I was in the perfect spot. I paddled into the wave, got under the lip, and pulled into the barrel. As I was traveling in the barrel, one of the Brazilian guests dropped in on me and ruined what would have been the wave of the day, for me. It wasn't just that I got completely worked by the wave after suffering from a concussion earlier that day, it was that this guy was cool to my face the whole trip then burned me on that wave, knowing how dangerous it is to drop in on someone. To be clear, I spent the day ensuring that each guest got plenty of waves and always made sure to coach them along the way. It's not only common but expected for surf guides to also participate in sessions, so me paddling into the wave wasn't taking away from the guests. It was just unnecessary and selfish, and that's surfing for you. It can be a very selfish sport. That's why my friends and I have spent so much time getting off the beaten path, going to areas with no one around.

All in, the trip was a dream. I had a newfound respect for Zane, who would spend six months straight in the Mentawais every year. The place is magic, but outside of surfing, there is absolutely nothing to do. There's the resort, the waves, and the jungle. I was thankful for the experience but also thankful not to live there full-time.

Get in, get some, get out.

[BINGIN BEACH, INDONESIA —FEBRUARY 2015]

Now that I wasn't working for Christian anymore, I had been spending a lot of time over at Jack's villa. There were always guys from home dropping in, searching for a reprieve from the grind of western society.

Brandon wasn't exactly that, but he was looking for something. I had known Brandon for some time. He was one of the most solid guys that I was lucky enough to meet in early sobriety, back when I had one year under my belt and he had four. He was one of the first guys I met who showed me you can be confident and funny without drugs and alcohol. Up until then, I hadn't really met anyone like that, and it really inspired me. He was fucking hilarious and really quick-witted. We became fast friends.

It always threw me that he was an atheist. Not just with Brandon, but in general, it has always triggered me when I've found out someone is an atheist. Just as it probably triggers them when they find out that I believe in God. I remember him thinking that anyone who believed in God was an idiot.

Other than that, he was great—a fellow surfer who was really into history and happened to teach high school in LA.

"So whatta you have going on at the moment?" Brandon said as I found myself thinking that he looked like he could easily be a member of Metallica. You know, long straight hair with a goatee, and the confidence that made him blind to what he actually looked like.

"Honestly, man, I just went through this big ordeal working with a friend. Immigration busted us for working without visas." I paused. "It scared the shit out of us but we learned a lot."

"Good that you learned something about doing business down here," Brandon said, pleased that I had teed him up nicely for his proposal. "I've been thinking that it would be a good time to open a sober living in Bali. I've got some money to play with, and I'm thinking you should run it while I'm in the States, and we'll go fifty-fifty?"

Brandon was a smart guy and, like me, he was looking for an opportunity to make money doing something we loved. He knew as well as I did that there is a lot of money in recovery, and he hated being a high school teacher.

"Really?" I asked. "Alright, let's play with some numbers and I'll start looking around for a villa."

Brandon and I agreed to go into business together. He made his way back to LA for the start of the school year and I went straight into searching for a property that could house our clients. It was a very simple business model: lease a property, make a website, get the word out.

Through a friend, I was able to find a brand-new luxury villa. It was a beautiful, modern home with three stories and a swimming pool, and each room had its own full bathroom with a big shower. The place was perfect. I quickly rang Brandon to let him know that I found our spot.

"Let's take it," he said, ready to hit the ground running.

That same day, Brandon took out a $20,000 loan. He had great credit, which worked to our advantage. He sent me the check, and I took it straight to the owner of the villa. Twenty thousand dollars in USD was close to 300 million Indonesian rupiah at the time. It worked out to be about $1,600 a month, which is unheard of in the States. A property like that in the US would cost a minimum of $10,000 per month. Now you know why so many people move to Bali.

We had the villa, but we didn't have any clients, so it was time to get the word out. This meant meeting people in recovery letting them know we had a location and were running a sober living. Brandon and I really had the best intentions; our goal was to provide a safe, sober environment, with structure for the clients, and to make money while doing it. It seemed like a lot of people are making money these days helping people, so why not us? We could be doing worse things in the world.

Like anything worthwhile, it took some time before we landed the first client, and we were definitely starting to feel the stress creeping in. We maintained our focus, kept meeting with new people, sharing our stories, and sharing our approach to the house. Our efforts paid off. The first client came, and after that, they just kept coming. Before we knew it, the house was full.

[SEMINYAK, INDONESIA —MAY 2015]

It was still the early days of running the sober living. I was relaxing, lying in bed resetting after a long day of work, when I got a text from Kendra.

Hey! What are you up to? Jessica tells me you're doing really well and that you're on your way to becoming a millionaire! LOL. I'm headed to Nusa Lembongan on Sunday, you wanna come?

I was surprised to see the text, and a bit confused since Kendra was dating Eric, a good friend of Christian's. I didn't know it then, but Kendra had recently broken up with him and had her sights set on me.

I texted back, *Things are going well and we're enjoying the work! I'm not able to make it this weekend but keep me in the loop. Thanks for the invite.*

A week or so later, Kendra was back from her trip and hit me up again. I was in a weird place in that time period as far as love goes. At that point, I had been sober for seven years and still hadn't had a real relationship. I hadn't had a quality woman come into my life. Probably because I hadn't become a quality man, and I was sorry and disappointed about that. I was tired of having flings or engaging in behavior that made me feel empty, alone, and unsafe. At the same time, while I wanted a relationship, I wasn't sure if Kendra was the right fit for me. I knew her to be someone who fed on drama, but she was into health and was striving to be a better person. That meant something to me. Still, I didn't want to create any bad blood with Eric.

I decided to go meet her and her friends at a local bar. The place was a typical Bali lounge. It was completely open to the elements, a roof but no real walls, and daybed-like sofas covered in colorful pillows. I made it a point to hug all the girls in the group to prevent any misinterpreted signs of interest or anything like that. I thought it would be nice to go out, socialize, and not be alone. I went out with the intention of just being friends with Kendra.

"So how's it going?"

"Ahhh, well, I'm not sure if you've heard, but Eric and I broke up."

"Really," I said, starting to piece it all together. "Sorry to hear that."

"Don't be. It was time. It got really unhealthy and needed to happen, so I've been letting loose and having fun." She grinned.

I hung out with the girls for a while, just talking and trying to have a good time. It was always hard when I was sober and everyone else was having drinks. At some point, as had become custom, I decided it was time for me to head home.

I said goodbye to everyone, jumped on my motorbike, and started my drive back. By the time I was almost there,

I saw a text from Kendra that said, *Hey, the girls bailed me, where are you?*

I pulled over and texted back, *Do you need a ride?*

Yes, she replied.

I'm not far away. I'll come back and get you now.

I pulled back up to the lounge.

"So your friends bailed you, huh?" I asked, knowing full well that she had ditched them, but willing to play along in her game. At this point, as nervous as I was about the situation, I was playing it too.

"Yeah, can I crash on your couch tonight?"

"Of course, that's fine. Jump on."

Kendra eagerly hopped on the back of the bike, and we took off into the Bali night.

We pulled up at my place; neither of us said much. I offered Kendra my hand and felt the warmth of her fingers clutch my palm as she stood up to dismount the bike. I opened the door and stepped to the side, letting Kendra walk in ahead of me.

As I entered the living room, I said, "Okay, so you can sleep on that couch. Let me grab you a blanket."

"Oh my god, the mosquitoes are going to annihilate me." She was right. All houses are outdoor in Bali and there was no mosquito net. "Do you mind if I sleep in your room?" she said, as if it was the most innocent question.

"Ahhh," I paused. Knowing all too well what would happen but convincing myself that I could behave and possibly just hold her until we fell asleep. I told myself that's as far as I would take it.

"That's fine," I responded.

Kendra walked into my room, and we were instantly

pulled together like magnets. With zero hesitation, we were kissing passionately.

Pulling myself away, I took a step back. "Oh wow...what are we doing?"

"I don't know, but it feels right," she said, putting her fingers through my own and pulling me back in for more.

The passion intensified quickly from there. I picked her up and carried her over to the bed. She was so light and petite, and I had so much blood rushing through my body, that it was easy. We went into a lovemaking time warp. It felt as though we had both been empty and alone our entire lives and were finally whole. Something I had never quite experienced.

Afterward, we laid in bed in awe.

Kendra broke the silence first. "What was that?"

"I don't know."

"That was the best sex of my life. It was beyond sex. I don't even know what to make of that," she said, curling her toes under the sheets as she spoke.

"Me neither," I responded, baffled as well and speechless.

Looking over at the clock, she said, "Holy shit! We went for six hours. I should head home."

"Okay, I'll give you a ride home."

We arrived at Kendra's as the sun was coming up. As she began to walk toward the path to her villa, I grabbed her hand. She spun toward me as I kissed her goodbye.

I knew I was in trouble. The ride back home was an absolute blur. I was replaying the entire evening in my mind from start to finish. I kept telling myself that this shouldn't happen, that it wasn't smart to go into a relationship with her, but it also felt so good to be with her.

[SEMINYAK, INDONESIA —FEBRUARY 2016]

Things were going really well with the facility. We were at full capacity and I was able to bring in a modest salary. It felt amazing to have built something of our own and even more amazing that we were genuinely helping people in the process. At the time, there was really only one main rehab in Bali. It was owned by an Australian guy who had a reputation for being a ruthless shark, as do most people in the recovery industry. This guy started to pursue Brandon and I for a partnership. We put up a bit of resistance and even turned him down at the start. The thing about Bali, though, you are never completely certain if everything is legal.

We were not a rehab, we were not treating people, but we were a sober living. Bad things happen in sober living homes all the time. People relapse, there are clashes in the house, and sometimes people even die. We were fortunate enough that it didn't happen at this home, but I have seen it happen at other places I have worked.

After everything that I went through with immigration, I was nervous and highly stressed that the owner of the rehab would call immigration on me to have us shut down and have me possibly go to jail. Reluctantly, after many meetings, Brandon and I decided that we would be better off entering into a partnership so we would at least be safe under his umbrella. Our agreement was that we would run and operate the sober living facility but he would take a cut and provide the infrastructure that we didn't have. Over time, things shifted. He started demanding that I work shifts in his rehab, which was not part of the deal. I didn't open a sober living to become this man's employee, and I had no intention of spending my free time working at his rehab.

Tensions increased rapidly, and part of me thinks that was his intention all along. When our one-year lease came to a close, we had already moved money into the joint account as part of the joint venture. At that point, he was able to take away our access to our money and prevented us from renewing our lease or renting a new location. This never would have flown in the States, but in so many parts of the world, things just don't operate the way we are used to. It's pretty clear to me now that he planned this from the start, but what really infuriates and saddens me is that our intent was pure. We were charging a modest rate, and we were really focused on helping our clients. For him, it was all about the money.

[DELHI, INDIA —MARCH 2016]

Ever since they were children, Christian and Jessica had followed a guru from India. Their parents had followed this guru for about thirty-five years, so it was only natural that they did as well. At the time, I was seeking. I had just read the story of Eben Alexander, a neurosurgeon who had a near-death experience or NDE. His story changed my world, and that's putting it lightly. I began to listen to more accounts of NDEs; there was something that drew me to their stories. I had always been open to God, but I didn't know that people were having experiences with the spirit world and that you could have similar experiences through meditation. Everything that Christian and Jessica had been sharing with me started to line up with what I was learning from these NDEs. This fascinated me, and I began meditating more and more and was actually getting results, experiencing more peace and trust in life overall. I had been spending so much time around Christian and Jessica, learning from them, and being exposed to their way of thinking. They were both very private about their spiritual path, but when they saw how this practice had changed me, they invited me to join them in India to stay at the ashram of the guru they followed.

We landed in Delhi. It was an assault on the senses, to put it mildly. Honestly, it is by far the most disgusting place I have ever been. It is considered one of, if not the, most polluted city on the planet. Everywhere you go smells horrible. There is a dust in the air that I swear you can taste. Everywhere you look there is trash and some of the most evil monkeys I have ever encountered. They have the look of a demon in their eyes and a violence to match.

We took the pothole-ridden dirt road through the city and made our way to the ashram. When we arrived, I was shocked to find a completely different world behind the gates. It was quiet, peaceful, and orderly. Everything was taken care of for us—food, shelter, all of it. The meditators practiced cooking and cleaning as a form of service to the ashram, myself included.

I admit that I wasn't convinced about the guru at the beginning. I have always been a bit of an open-minded skeptic. It was hard for me to believe in things without experiencing them for myself. However, one day, while we were in a meditation with thousands of Indians, I had what you might call a paranormal experience with this guru.

All of the visitors were put in the front rows of the meditation hall. The meditation was in Hindi but we were given headphones so we could listen to the English translation. You would sometimes wait for hours before the guru would actually show up. This was one of those instances. There I was, sitting in the front of this massive meditation room with thousands of people, and all I could think about was how badly I had to pee. I decided to get up and make my way to the bathroom, hoping I could get back before the guru showed up to start the show. As luck would have it, the guru showed up while I was peeing and got started. Once he starts, you're not allowed to walk through the crowd or in front of anyone, so there was no way I was going to be able to get back to my seat or get my headphones for the translation.

I was going through so much mental anguish at the time. I was newly seeing Kendra and was stressing out about it. Christian and Jessica kept telling me I shouldn't date her. They knew my past, and they knew that I needed a good woman by my side. They liked Kendra as a friend, but they knew she was addicted to drama, and it didn't help that Christian was good friends with her ex. Truth be told, they had my best interest at heart. Still, this really rattled me.

I was dealing with a lot of anger, and when I couldn't get back to my seat, I sort of exploded with rage in my mind. I was desperate to hear what this guru had to say, and I was hoping that I could get some guidance in my life through his wisdom since it seemed Christian and Jessica gained so much from following his work.

As the guru began speaking, in Hindi, I was sitting toward the back of the meditation hall just off to the side. My anger was building, and I almost left the gathering, thinking I would walk around the local village and blow off some steam. Earlier in the trip, one of the followers told me to focus on the guru, no matter what, just put all my attention on him. So I stayed. I sat down and, even though I couldn't understand a word he was saying, I put all my attention on him. After ten to fifteen minutes of doing this, I don't know how else to explain this, but I was completely lifted out of my rage and found myself in a state of peace and bliss. It was like the whole room and my mind went quiet. It felt as though I was lifted into another dimension with the guru and that he was communicating with me telepathically. He told me to let go of all my little problems and to focus on my connection with him. It was very simple yet profound; it felt like I had taken drugs, and I was in a state of bliss for the rest of the day.

I don't know what this guru's intent is in this world, and I'm not a follower of his, but I know he has power.

[SOLANA BEACH, CA —JUNE 2016]

I came back to California to help get my dad into a treatment center. At this point, he had been homeless for years and couldn't stop drinking. He was depressed, suicidal, and beaten down by a lifetime of pain, but something was different. For the first time, he expressed a willingness to get sober. It was because of that willingness that I decided to fly back to California to try and help him get into a treatment program. Mind you, I wasn't necessarily in the most stable position in general, but I figured I had enough contacts in the recovery space that I could find something for him. I really thought that, but I was wrong.

After landing, I went straight to reaching out to facilities. I spoke to over thirty treatment centers, and no one would take him. I exhausted all of my recovery contacts—literally anyone who I thought could help out—and nothing. I was furious, enraged. Here's my dad, who has been homeless for years now, finally expressing some willingness to get sober again, and I can't find anything for him. Whether it was that the facility wouldn't accept his HMO insurance or that he was in the process of detoxing methadone, which is the hardest and longest detox process of any drug, or the fact that they were looking to charge $30,000 to $40,000 minimum per month for treatment, it was all another form of "No."

Trying to get my dad into rehab showed the very real, dark side of the recovery industry. Once again, it's all about money. The people who work in the facilities actually care about people, for the most part, but the owners—the owners are almost always vultures.

After failing to secure a place for my dad, what do you think he did next? He did exactly what he knew best: started drinking again.

I was so defeated, so angry. It lit a fire in me to want to create something for addicts who don't have the resources to afford treatment. One day, God willing.

[SOUTH OF FRANCE —JULY 2016]

I arrived in Paris straight from the States. I was still in a pretty raw headspace after everything I had just gone through with my dad. I made my way to the train station and boarded a train to the South of France to meet Kendra and her family for her sister Claire's wedding. Between the flight and the train, it was a long trip.

Kendra's soon-to-be brother-in-law rented out an entire hotel. It was historic, ancient really, and beyond beautiful. There's something remarkable about seeing structures like this. It stops you in your tracks. The detail of the stonework, the shape of the building itself, we don't get to see things like that in California. All of the buildings in my hometown were put up in the last one hundred years or less. They are pretty much all low-level, stucco buildings without any character or soul to them. Being in France, looking at this hotel, reminded me of how rich human history really is. It also made me stop and think to myself, *Who the hell rents out an entire hotel?* Come to find out, billionaires. Her sister was marrying an actual billionaire, and he laid out roughly ten million dollars for this wedding.

Experiencing a wedding like this was a once-in-a-lifetime opportunity, but man was I a fish out of water. I felt so awkward most of the time. Cruising around with billionaire sheiks who have an air of superiority isn't really my scene. As I mentioned earlier, I have a hard time with arrogant people who act superior to other humans. My heroes have always been people who are the best at what they do but still have the humility to treat others as equals.

After the wedding, we decided to drive over to Hosseger to explore the coast and get some surf. Kendra was always on board to do anything I wanted to do. I had a friend who was living there, working for a well-known surf brand. He was living what seemed like a really cool but simple life. We stayed with him and his wife and explored the coast for a bit before heading back to Avignon.

When we got back, we arrived to drama. Kendra's sister was upset that we had decided to leave and go to the coast. She said it was a special time for family, and we just bailed. I thought to myself, *Why didn't she say anything before we left*? I never understood people who weren't up front about their feelings. I was so uncomfortable around everyone that I really wanted to take a break, and like I said, Kendra was more than willing to go along with it. Still, I felt bad pushing for us to go on the trip and for creating drama between them. There was always drama between Kendra and her sisters.

People can get addicted to drama. Myself included.

When all was said and done, I had bigger problems to solve. When the trip ended, I flew back to California to have one last crack at helping my dad.

I felt defeated. No matter how hard I tried, I couldn't get

my dad into a treatment program. By now, he was drinking again and seemed to have entirely given up hope of getting sober. As crushing as it was, I made the decision to go back home to Bali and to Kendra.

[DUBAI —DECEMBER 2016]

Kendra and I were spending time in Dubai with her family. We were staying at her sister Claire's house, but everyone was there, her mom and her other sisters. The home was something out of a magazine, but then again, that was to be expected after the wedding we went to. I could never get used to this level of affluence. It felt over the top and stifling at the same time. I always felt like an imposter.

We spent most of our time with the family. Claire had just given birth to her first baby, so we all took turns helping out, holding the baby, and catching up. It was nice to be with family—well, to be with her family. I got along really well with her mom, and I respected how hard she worked to take care of her girls.

Even though we were having a good time, it was long days with the family. One night, we headed back to our room early for a bit of solace. As we sat up in bed, I could feel the tension building within Kendra. Her shoulders began to hunch inward; her jaw tightened, eyes blinking more slowly.

Tears fell from Kendra's eyes as she turned to me and said, "I feel so happy and sad at the same time."

Concerned and wanting to support her, I said, "Talk to me. I'm here."

The tears continued to fall as she spoke. "When I was sixteen, someone slipped me a date rape pill. When I was unconscious..." She paused, exhaling deeply as she held her eyes shut for a moment. "Well, I ended up getting pregnant and having an abortion. Every time I hold Claire's baby, I can't help but think that I killed a little baby. I keep thinking that the baby would be grown by now."

My heart broke for her. "I'm so sorry." There was nothing more I could say other than, "I'm here, okay? I love you."

I couldn't imagine the pain she felt, both back then and here in this moment, all these years later. All I could do was to be there for her and to love her.

I held her for some time. I felt her body begin to soften and calm. I brushed her hair away from her face, tucking the golden lock behind her ear as I kissed her cheek, letting the salt of her tears soak my lips. We began to kiss. Kendra made her way on top of me, sticking her tongue in my mouth, and putting me inside of her. We made passionate love like we always did.

"I love you," she said as she continued kissing me.

"I love you too," I responded as the sex intensified. There was only a thin wall between our room and her mother's. I did my best to keep the volume at a respectable level, but I'm not sure we managed to do that.

She kept riding me, getting lost in the act, which I always loved.

"I'm getting close," I said, surprised to feel her continuing—clamping down as I orgasmed.

I knew what she was doing, and part of me invited it. Up until that point, I had had such a crazy life, so much pain and loneliness. I wanted to experience what it was like to be a father, to have a family of my own, and part of me wanted to give her what she had lost. I wanted to be the one to give her that gift. Everything seemed right, and we loved each other.

Kendra sensually kissed me as she dismounted and lay motionless in bed with her eyes closed.

"Oh my God, I'm seeing golden spirals. I think I just got pregnant."

I laughed lightly, thinking she must be hallucinating, but happy to go along with it. "Well, let's welcome their little soul in," I said.

[UBUD, INDONESIA —JANUARY 2017]

The sun had just come up and was hitting the ocean in a way that made it glitter. I was checking the surf when I saw Kendra walking through the meadow toward me. Morning light streamed through as she was surrounded by the green fields of Bali, making her look like a blonde angel. She held a cup of tea with both hands as she stepped through the grass, a big smile stretching across her face.

"I'm pregnant."

Immediately overcome with excitement and joy, "You knew it," I said, hugging her tightly before stepping back and looking into her eyes. "We're doing this."

"We're doing this!" she said, smiling while she giggled.

We were both so happy, you could feel the energy between us. I remember holding her from behind as we both laughed, looking out at the sea.

Later that day, Christian and Jessica came by to visit. We couldn't wait to share the news with them. I honestly thought they would share in our happiness. I knew Christian wasn't always the biggest fan of our relationship, but I really thought

Kendra being pregnant was a gift, and that they would share in that feeling. They did their best to feign excitement, but I could tell immediately. The two of them were going through a difficult time with their own kid. They knew the realities of having a baby and they were genuinely concerned for us.

"Are you guys sure this is a good idea?" Jessica asked as Christian looked on intently.

Kendra jumped in first. "We're so excited," she said, as if there was no room for any other emotion and certainly no room for any other questions or negative attitudes.

"It's crazy; Kendra knew she was pregnant right away. But yeah, we're so happy and ready for it. We can't wait."

Kendra and Jessica got talking, and I stepped outside with Christian, eager to get some time to chat with him privately.

"So," I started in right away, "how has your experience been, becoming a father?"

Christian took a deep breath before speaking. "It's been beautiful but very difficult as well."

"Oh yeah? In what way?" I asked, surprised to hear him admit that they struggled. They seemed like such natural parents to me.

"It brings up a lot of stuff from childhood. It's made things difficult between Jessica and I." Looking over his shoulder to make sure we were alone, he continued. "Sometimes I think I would have been better off not having a kid," he said with a painful chuckle. "I love my child, don't get me wrong; I just didn't expect for it to be this hard or for so many things to come up because of it. I thought I worked through all my demons when I went through the Twelve Steps, but this was something different, something I didn't even know existed. You know, some generational shit from when I was a kid."

It won't be that hard, I thought to myself. Boy was I in for a surprise.

[UBUD, INDONESIA —MAY 2017]

Kendra was close to six months pregnant. We were having a beautiful and peaceful pregnancy. We would surf together, Kendra paddling on her knees into soft rolling waves, our daughter bound to love the ocean.

One day, I was relaxing at home. It was just one of those lazy moments where you're bored but you don't really want to do anything. There was no real reason to do it. I was on Kendra's computer, on her Facebook account, and I was curious. That combination of bored and curious where you just start aimlessly looking up old friends, exes, anyone you've ever known. It was harmless, I wasn't looking because I was interested in one of my exes or anything like that. I hadn't been home in ages, and I just wanted to see what everyone from home was doing.

I really loved Kendra during this period. She had my whole heart. I was so happy to be with her, and the fact that we were bringing a kid into this world was amazing. For me, I felt like everything was finally coming together. I was about to have a family of my own. I had absolutely no intention of cheating or anything like that.

I don't think Kendra saw it that way.

She went through my search history and turned something innocent into a massive blowup.

There were some major insecurities that I had unknowingly triggered. I unleashed a deep trauma and an absolute monster that came with it. Kendra told me that she already had trust issues because of her ex. She explained that during her first serious relationship, she was with a French athlete back in Dubai. They had been together for over a year and talked about getting married. Apparently, out of nowhere, he ghosted her. One day he just stopped talking to her and she never saw him again. Somehow, she ended up finding out that he was actually engaged to another woman the entire time they were together. It traumatized her and magnified any insecurities she already had.

It was almost like she was taking out her anger at him on me. It turned into an explosive fight with no reprieve in sight. No matter what I said, she just wouldn't let up. She kept saying that I didn't really love her and was threatening to have an abortion. I couldn't believe that something so innocent could escalate into threatening the life of our unborn child. I felt like I needed to walk away, and that's exactly what I did. I left the house for a couple of nights to let things settle. I kept trying to make it clear to her that this was unnecessary and that I loved her completely.

With time, we were able to make peace. We were engaged at the time and were moving forward with getting married.

Our plan was to go to Australia to do all of the paperwork and have a wedding later.

We flew down to Australia as planned. As we sat in front of the clerk at the registration office, Kendra revealed that she had mysteriously forgotten all of the documents back in Bali. Without the papers, we couldn't get married, and she knew that. She pulled the dumb blonde card, leaning heavily on the fact that she was always known as a bit of a bonehead. I didn't know what to think as I was filled with a rush of confusion and numbness.

I know now that she left the paperwork in Bali on purpose. She later told me that she never forgave me for the Facebook search. For her, in that moment, that was it, we were done.

[BALI HOSPITAL —AUGUST 2017]

Kendra's mom, Vickie, flew in for the birth of our daughter. I remember always being taken aback and impressed by Vickie, by her strength. She and Kendra were twins in appearance. Vickie had strong alpha energy. She is a die-hard feminist, absolutely hates men although she rarely shows it, and focuses most of her time on building her business. She is an entrepreneur, starting her own business in the Middle East, an otherwise male-dominated culture where very few women have succeeded on their own.

So here I was in the birthing room with Kendra and her mom. The energy was intense, to say the least.

Kendra was struggling. This wasn't how we planned it. Our plan was to have a water birth. We wanted our little girl to be born at home in the most peaceful way possible. For us, water just seemed like the natural solution for that. Labor, like being a parent, turned out to be much more difficult than expected. There were so many of us in the room, we completely filled the space, absorbing each other's energy both with excitement and fear. The energy was made all the more palpable by the rare eclipse that happened to be taking place at that very moment.

After hours of intense pain and little progress, Kendra was ready to give in. She wanted a natural birth more than anything; we had talked about it, and I knew she would regret the epidural. Immediately after she requested it, I pulled the doctor aside. I asked him to give me thirty minutes to try something, and he obliged.

I put on Beethoven's "Moonlight Sonata." Immediately, Kendra's breathing slowed. It was as if the music did something to her. It calmed her yet gave her the strength she needed to withstand the pain. The song played on repeat, nonstop. Everyone in the room was ready to snap if they heard it play one more time, but not Kendra. The song was the only thing that soothed her.

The Indonesian doctor was gentle with Kendra. "Okay. Push. Push. Good, now breathe."

Kendra screamed endlessly, tears running down her face.

I looked over at Vickie; she was crying as well.

"You've got it. You've got it. I love you," I kept saying as she pushed.

"Come, come," the doctor waved me over as the head was beginning to crown. "You catch."

As River came out, I was there to catch her. She fell right into my arms. I was the first person in this world to hold her. Immediately, I was overcome with a rush of emotions. I couldn't believe how beautiful she was. I had been so worried that she would come out looking like me because I always felt that I would make for one ugly woman, but there she was. She looked exactly like me, and somehow she was the most beautiful thing I'd ever seen. I couldn't look away. Our little girl was perfect, and I was relieved and grateful to finally have a family of my own.

~ ~ ~

The family was there to greet us when we pulled up to the villa. They helped us bring everything inside, giving us a chance to introduce River to our home peacefully. That's exactly what our home was, an incredibly peaceful and beautiful place set on the rice patties.

"You guys did so well. I am so proud of you, Kendra," Vickie said.

Gently smiling, looking up as she breastfed River, "Thank you, mum."

"Isn't she beautiful," I said, more of a statement than a question.

"Yes, she looks just like you, Mikey," Vickie responded.

After Vickie went home, the real world set in. The first few days were an absolute blur. We were quickly learning how hard it was to look after an infant on our own. Kendra became hyperworried about every little thing. River was just nine days old when she caught her first cold. We were both worried, but Kendra was in a complete state of panic. She was so beyond overcome with fear and anxiety over River having a cold. It was to the point where she couldn't function. There was no talking to her, no reasoning with her; it was a complete mental shutdown.

"Is she going to be okay?" Kendra asked, the fear spilling out of her with every breath.

"Kendra, she has a cold; she isn't going to die," I said to her, trying to find the balance between letting her know I was being supportive, but also that she seemed to be acting overly dramatic.

"I'm sorry; I'm just worried about her. She's so young," Kendra said, shaking in terror.

There was nothing else I could say. I kept silent but I couldn't help myself from thinking she was creating way too much unnecessary stress for something as minor as a cold. Of course, I was worried, I wanted my baby to be healthy, but adding stress to situations never helps, and I was sure River was picking up on that. Over the years, I had learned to stay calm in calamity, perhaps too calm.

My sense of calm was short-lived. I quickly became a distressed father. I felt everything piling up on me. Kendra and I were in the middle of building a boutique lodge. We had taken a loan out to build the property, which included ten rooms, a café, a yoga shala, and a pool, an ideal space for retreats. I was spending most of my days working on-site, navigating construction, red tape, and corruption at the local level. Things at home weren't much better; as I felt that I had lost Kendra entirely, she had become a different person overnight with her constant anxiety. I know that it's normal for a mother to love and worry about her child, but this was different.

Our approach to parenting couldn't be more opposite. Kendra had grown up with a silver spoon. She had been smothered with love and appeasement to ensure she was always happy. On the other hand, I was neglected entirely, raised with unhealthy forms of discipline. There's speculation of physical abuse. I have had unexplained scars since I was a kid. Looking back, I struggle to remember; in fact, I don't have any memories before the age of seven. My brain has done a good job of trying to protect me from what I can only imagine was hell for a kid.

Kendra's level of anxiety over every little thing sent me into a tailspin. It triggered something in me that I didn't know existed. I'm not trying to paint Kendra in a bad light; I am trying to educate on what a toxic relationship looks like. We attracted each other through our trauma. It was as if we were magnetized by it. Our traumas were at the opposite ends of the spectrum, but the same level of wounding nonetheless. All of that baggage spilled out the moment we had River. It was as though we could only see the negative in each other from that moment on. I wasn't jealous of my daughter; that's not what it was. I was so angry that I lost my partner because of the paralyzing anxiety the baby was causing her.

A few weeks after River came down with a cold, Kendra came home to find me sitting in the bedroom, crying.

"What's going on, Mikey?" Kendra said, shocked to see me this way.

Amid tears, I responded, "I don't understand what is happening. River was crying, and I got carried away trying to quiet her down. I couldn't stop screaming at her." I paused, taking in gulps of air. "I couldn't control myself; it was like something came over me and I just couldn't stop."

There are really no words to explain this, no amount of therapy to understand what I was doing. It felt like—and still, to this day, it feels like—I was possessed. I know it's easy to say that, to say I don't know what happened, to say it wasn't me, but somehow it was me. I treated my daughter, the person I loved the most in the world, the way I was treated. When I would cry as a child I was screamed at, squeezed, and pinched rather than comforted. It doesn't make it right and it's not an excuse, but that's exactly what I did, and I hated myself for it.

I had sworn I would never turn out like my dad, someone who would belittle, antagonize, and torment the ones he loved. But here I was, doing the same things he had done. These traits were passed down to me through the environment and the frequency my family created.

"It's okay, Mikey. We'll work through it," she said, walking over to sit next to me on the bed. She put her arm around me as she said, "It's going to be okay. I love you."

Maybe she knew, maybe she didn't, but it was not okay.

~ ~ ~

Listen, it's not easy for me to be honest about all of this. I'm trying to provide awareness for someone who may have had a tumultuous childhood—to know what may come up for them after having a child. I was in the dark about all of this. I'm at the point where I don't give a fuck if someone judges me for this, because I've been through so much pain that in many ways, it feels like a part of me has already died.

I was a distressed dad who crumbled under the pressure. I don't think I should suffer for the rest of my life for that. What eats at me the most is that I wasn't a perfect dad. I had this idea that I would be a perfect, loving father who never got angry or overreacted. Most of my guilt comes from not meeting that expectation of myself.

If you did have a horrible childhood, get help before you

have children. Make sure you have a community around you. It will be the most important thing you do. In the old days, children were raised by the tribe; these days it seems like the family unit is set up to fail. Look at the higher rates of divorce and family units falling apart; it's insanity. Kendra and I didn't have one family member around us full time. We were completely isolated in Bali. It would've taken massive amounts of pressure off both of us to have a strong community around us.

I've never heard anyone talk about the things that I am talking about the way that I am talking about them, and I don't understand why. Look how sick our world is. Look at all of the tortured souls that you see on a daily basis, people living on the streets who've turned to drugs, crime, and a tormented life. Most of the time, these are people who were fucked up as kids, abused by the people who loved them most, and they don't know what happened.

Do you think that my parents, at their core, wanted to be abusive? No, the abuse was passed down to them in a frequency; that frequency was passed down to me, and I did my best not to, but some of that frequency was passed down to my daughter. Yes, there are sadistic people in the world, but my parents weren't like that. They were, and still are, good people at heart; they just had really fucked-up childhoods that led to them repeating the same cycle as their parents and likely their grandparents before them.

[UBUD, INDONESIA —2017–2018]

It is said that Bali is an energetic portal in the world. It is also said that there is something magical in Bali that supports you and carries you if you are in the right flow, but if you are not, it will destroy you. I learned firsthand how true this is.

As my fuse quickened and my temper became more and more uncontrollable, it spread from trying to quiet River to lashing out at Kendra. I saw the patterns emerging, but I could do nothing to stop it. For the most part, when River and I were alone together, it was pure bliss. I loved every moment with her as I lost myself just looking into her big brown eyes. But for some reason, whenever Kendra was with us, the demon residing inside of me came out. I don't even think she knew she was doing it, but Kendra had this way of creating anxiety, panic, and drama that made it feel like I had to scream my way into silencing it. Everything became a fight; there was nothing sacred or off-limits.

Throughout my life, even in sobriety, I have been plagued by suicidal thinking. This period was no different, other than it too was amplified.

The voice in my mind was constantly screaming, *KILL YOURSELF! KILL YOURSELF! KILL YOURSELF! KILL YOURSELF!* This went on for a week straight.

I tried to seek help, going from one place to another. I was determined to understand why I was lashing out like this, and how to stop myself. I was willing to do anything to keep my family together. At this point, my efforts weren't mirrored by my partner. Kendra had convinced me that it was my fault, that I was the problem.

When you are in a bad headspace, it feels like everything is working against you. In Bali, a world away from home, this feeling was amplified.

Mirroring my energy or as a form of payback for how I treated my daughter, the ocean took out its aggression on me. In the past, I had surfed these waves with grace, but lately, it was wipeout after wipeout, my body getting wrecked on the reef. I would come out with gashes, blood running down my body.

We were still living together and building the lodge. Our home was on the property, which meant there was no separation. I would leave the house after a fight and walk out to the construction site to begin working. Dealing with Indonesians on a daily basis became hell. Bartering in broken English became infuriating, and I felt like everyone I came across was lying to me or trying to rip me off. I would get on my motorbike to try and escape, only to be stuck in hours of traffic and pollution, screaming and cursing at myself inside my helmet.

[CANGGU, INDONESIA —MAY 2018]

It's funny, I never realized you could hit rock bottom so hard while being sober. I can't even imagine how unbearable this would have been if I added drinking to the mix. This must have been what my parents experienced.

After an endless sea of healers and self-loathing, I found myself sitting in Sherry's Healing Room. I had completely lost hope in understanding what was happening to me; in figuring out why I was getting so angry at someone I loved so much. So there I was, face-to-face with Sherry.

Sherry was a somatic healer and intuitive guide. When we met, she was dressed in all white. Come to think of it, she always wore all white, which contributed to her looking like a white witch. She was originally from Australia, in her late fifties with dark soulful brown eyes and blonde hair that was beginning to fade into creamy white. Sherry had an incredible energy that was strong and spiritual but also very supportive and genuinely compassionate. Nonjudgmental.

"So, Mike, I'm so glad we could make this happen. What can I do for you?" She paused. "What are you here for?" she asked kindly, clearly able to tell I was in a fragile space as she began the session.

"Well," I said, collecting myself, "I'm in a very difficult situation. I am in the process of losing my family."

Leaning in, she gently commanded, "Tell me more."

"My partner, Kendra, and I have a one-year-old daughter. Her name is River, and she is everything I have ever hoped for. I don't quite understand it, but I've been horrible toward her. I wanted her so badly. I wanted to be the best father, the one I never had, and here I am, repeating history." Tears began to fill my eyes as I took a deep breath, willing myself to continue. "I really don't know what to say or even how to explain it, but it has been the most painful experience of my life. I've gone to countless people seeking help, and nothing has worked." Again, I paused, refusing to let myself succumb to the lump that had lodged itself in my throat. "I am here because I need help. I don't know what to do, but I know that if I don't make changes soon, I'm going to lose my family."

Taken aback, Sherry commented, "Okay, Mike, wow. I'm so sorry. Can I just say that I admire your honesty. Normally, I have to pry the truth out of people, and it can take weeks or months. The fact that you showed up here and shot straight from the hip is massive. Thank you."

"I'm in recovery, so I'm pretty used to being honest. It's part of the process."

"That's great, Mike. So tell me more about your story. How long have you been sober?"

I was comfortable with this line of questioning. I had been sharing my story of sobriety ever since I first stepped into AA. "I've been sober for over eight years. I come from a long line of alcoholics and addicts on both sides of the family. My family has suffered from a lot of abuse, neglect, suicide, death—you name it, this family has seen it."

We went deep in our first session. For the first time, I felt heard. I felt like she might be the only one who could help me. She had amazing references, and it seemed like she was genuinely looking to know me and to help me rather than to judge me. I continued to see Sherry for some time, unable to mend my family just yet, but determined to make it work, determined to fix it.

[CEMAGI, INDONESIA —OCTOBER 2018]

Things with Kendra spiraled out of control.

Our fights became more frequent. You name it, we fought about it. Some days I would come home to Kendra screaming that I had done nothing, nothing to contribute to building the lodge or to helping her at home with River. This was baffling to me. I was waking up at four thirty in the morning to lead surf coaching for retreats to keep an income flowing in before coming back to work on the property until nightfall. Other days we fought about other women. I wasn't interested in these women, but if she saw me notice a woman in town, she would go off about how she wasn't good enough. She would turn it into something weird, saying, "You know you could be with someone better, right? It's okay if you want to be with other women, I'm okay with it," almost encouraging me to do it. I never wanted to, and I never took her up on it, but that doesn't mean that she didn't stray herself. At this point, I was so rattled and so codependent that I would ask her over and over again until she admitted it.

In an act of desperation, I reached out to Christian for

advice. The first words out of his mouth were, "I tried to tell you."

Christian suggested that Kendra and I go to couples therapy. He said that when things got tough for him and Jessica, they went to a counselor and she really helped them. He told me that it gave him a safe space to call Jessica out on her bullshit and that the therapist backed him, which ultimately led to them working through some difficult issues. When he told me this, I was in.

Reluctantly Kendra agreed to go with me. What I hadn't realized is that we would each see the counselor individually first before sitting down together. I made it clear that I wanted to work things out; Kendra felt differently.

We sat down in the room, the three of us together.

The counselor spoke first. "So, Mike, Kendra has made it clear that she is 100 percent done."

I froze before beginning to shake with fear.

"You need to accept this, and it's what's best for you and your healing process right now."

She continued to explain that I was experiencing codependency, which I admit I was. As an addict, my partners turned into my drug, and I would go through a massive withdrawal process when losing them. It's love addiction.

The counselor continued, "Even if she comes back into your life right now, it's just you getting your drug and prolonging your healing. You need to be okay on your own before being together again, whether it's with Kendra or with someone else."

By the time we got home, it was clear that I needed to look for my own place.

"It's temporary, Mikey," Kendra assured me. "We need this. This is going to be good for you, and for us. Once you're in a good space, we can come back together healed. We are still going to see each other all the time with River."

The thought of moving out, of being away from River, broke me, but I trusted Kendra that we would be able to be together again.

I found myself a place outside of Canggu, tucked into the quiet rice patties.

[ULUWATU BEACH, INDONESIA —MARCH 2019]

By the time 2019 rolled around, I was a disaster. Sober, but a disaster.

Being separated from my family was the deepest, darkest period of my life, and that says a lot given my past and how many deep, dark periods I have walked through. I was wasting away, weighing in at 148 pounds, hardly eating and sleeping even less. I was having such debilitating panic attacks that I found myself smoking two packs of cigarettes a day, and I don't even smoke.

The reality of my situation, of losing my family, repeating my parents' mistakes, of being abandoned, caused a never-ending cycle of terror. It felt like there was no escape from a life of immense pain. Somehow, throughout all of this, I continued surfing. I can say with confidence, surfing was the only thing that kept me alive. Even though I was painfully thin and running on almost no energy, I just kept going.

One afternoon, while heading out to surf Uluwatu, I ran into an old friend, Jake.

"Hey, Mikey." He paused. "It's me, Jake," he said, realizing I didn't recognize him.

"Oh hey, Jake, what's up? How've you been?"

"Holy shit, you've lost weight, man?" he said, somewhere between concerned and a question.

Filled with shame, just utterly embarrassed, I replied, "Yeah, I've been surfing a lot."

"Wow, well, I'm headed over to Deserts tomorrow for the swell; maybe you should come? You got my number, right?"

"Okay, yeah, for sure. I'll hit you up," I answered, knowing full well I had no intention of following up with him. "Good to see you," I said, running out toward the surf.

Thinking back, I really looked unwell. Everyone noticed it. I was a walking billboard for loss, depression, and fear.

Not long after I ran into Jake, I bumped into this Aussie dude I knew both through surfing and recovery. Andrew had to be in his late sixties by now but was still in good shape from surfing all the time. He wore Ray-Ban reading glasses and had long, straight hair that was always covered with a hat. He was just one of those guys who was really cool, spiritual, and incredibly supportive—likely a product of years of sobriety.

"Hey, Andrew," I said, a bit more defeated than I intended.

"Mikey!" he said, excited to see me. "How you been, bro? You've lost weight!"

I was embarrassed, but I knew there was no use hiding it from him, so I explained, "I've been in a bad way. I'm in the process of losing my family." I took a moment to regain my composure. "I can't eat or sleep—I've been like this for months."

Looking me right in the eyes, he said, "Aww shit, dude. I'm so sorry." I knew he genuinely meant it.

"Yeah, it's been the most brutal thing I've ever walked through. I don't even know what to do," I admitted.

"I know people always act like they know how you feel, but man, I get it. I went through it at fifteen years sober. Almost killed me."

"Really?" I asked, surprised by his reciprocation of honesty.

"Yeah, it was the hardest thing I've ever walked through in my life. I lost everything. I was sleeping on a mate's lounge, lost thirty kilos, and woke up at 4:00 a.m. every day for a year."

Relieved to hear someone else had experienced the same thing, I replied, "That's exactly what is happening to me."

"Yeah, mate, I feel for ya. It's literally like part of you is dying, and that's because it is."

"So what do I do? How do I get through this?" I asked, desperate for answers.

"I have a book for ya that describes exactly what you're going through. Come to mine later, and I'll give you a copy. It will help give you an understanding of what is going on. This is all related to childhood stuff," Andrew said as he put his hand on my shoulder, showing support. "Other than that, you just need to ride through the pain. It may not seem like it, but you're actually healing right now."

"Holy shit! Seriously, thank you, Andrew. I'm not kidding you, I was about to drive my motorbike off a cliff."

"I almost did too."

It's hard to put into words how grateful you feel when you come across someone who has overcome similar pain. It's a beacon of light, of hope, and in that moment, I desperately needed hope.

[CANGGU, INDONESIA —APRIL 2019]

I continued to do everything I could to understand my past, to unlock and release the trauma of my youth. I looked for answers in books like the one Andrew gave me and continued working with Sherry as often as I could. It wasn't solving everything for me, it didn't allow me to go back in time and do things over, it didn't take away my pain, but it was allowing me to begin to understand it. For me, in that moment, beginning to understand the pain was enough to keep me hanging on.

Sherry had this incredible ability to know exactly where in my body healing was necessary, or maybe it was where my body would most easily allow the healing energy to enter. Over a lifetime of survival, I had built impenetrable armor without even realizing it. Sherry found an entry point to where I was holding the most painful of memories in my body. Through touch, energy work, and spiritual guidance, she navigated the turmoil with kindness and deep compassion.

During one particular session, Sherry was doing energy work on my body. It was physically more painful than I could ever have imagined.

I remember moaning in a way that built up into a scream.

"Stay with me, Mike. Stay with me," Sherry said soothingly while I continued to scream uncontrollably. "Yes! Go there! Go there, Mike!" she encouraged.

She was having a vision, and so she continued, "Oh Mike. I see you as a young boy. Your parents are addicts. They are abusing you, neglecting you. They starve you and treat you like a dog. They even put their cigarettes out on you."

I said nothing. I just laid there crying.

"I'm afraid you didn't make it past the age of three in that life." She paused. "Your parents left you for dead in a dumpster. That experience was stored in the blueprint of your soul and has been expressing itself in this life. This is what you have been fighting."

I was exhausted, completely drained, crying on the floor with images of River flashing through my mind.

Sherry said nothing. She laid there and held me the way a mother would, eventually returning to the physical treatment as she massaged my hand.

"You have a major block here, Mike," she said, pressing into the joint of my left thumb.

I screamed in pain before telling her, "I broke that thumb in the fifth grade, and it's been double-jointed ever since. How did you know?"

"It's what your body is showing me. Work with me here," she said, as she applied more pressure, resulting in my continued screaming.

Sherry worked various pressure points throughout my body, and eventually, I saw fire in my mind's eye as Sherry dropped to the floor in convulsions. It was unlike anything I had ever seen—she was floundering on the floor in a complete trancelike state. Trust me, I know how this sounds, but that's exactly what happened.

When she came to, she seemed completely blissed out, like coming out of the best meditation or drug trip you could ever imagine. She spoke softly, "Mike, your ancestors came. They did a healing on you. I was with them." She smiled. "Oh my God, I love being in that space."

Coming back to reality myself, "I could see fire," I said.

She began to tell me about the next vision she had. "In another life, you were a young Native American man, about eighteen years old. White people came and destroyed your people, leading you to become full of rage and hatred. You sought out the assistance of a dark medicine man. You made some sort of contract with this man that would allow you to do black magic and make white people very ill. This contract has been looming over you for many lifetimes. The contract was lifted here today." She continued, "Your ancestors said the closest you've been to your home in this lifetime is Montana."

I was speechless for a period of time. When I finally found the ability to speak, I said, "I used to live in Montana as a kid. My mom's tribe is from North Dakota."

"Wow, Mike. Congratulations," she said, acting as if this was a monumental moment for me.

Looking back, I don't know if I necessarily believed in everything she was telling me, but at that time, it was all I had to hold on to, and it also made it clear to me that there are people in this world who are connected to spiritual realms. I was in such a raw emotional state, in such a deep darkness, that I couldn't find the light on my own. I was desperate to heal, desperate to have my family back.

[TURTLE MOUNTAIN, ND —JULY 2019]

I felt like I needed to learn more about my ancestors in order to truly start healing from the intergenerational trauma I was uncovering. I never mentioned anything about my Native American heritage to Sherry, yet she knew all about it. She said there was something for me there and that I needed to connect with my roots when the time was right. For me, this meant now.

When I was younger, my mom had told me that we were Native American, but I never thought much about it. As I got older and started traveling more, I became interested. There was something about seeing how people loved and resonated with Native American culture that sparked something in me. In Bali, you'll see people selling all sorts of Native American–inspired pieces from headdresses to artifacts. There's a fascination with the culture. I think it's because Native Americans represent freedom and the notion of being deeply connected with and living in harmony with nature. People see what present-day colonialism has done to the world, and in many aspects, they hate it. I'm not saying it's all bad, but humanity could learn a lot from Native Americans, and I think people wish they could go back in time and learn rather than destroy.

So when I was back in the US, I took a chance to do just that, to learn. I had some things to take care of in California and knew I needed to visit the tribe. I drove up to North Dakota, just on the border of Canada. It was the longest drive of my life. I felt like I was driving to the edge of the world. My mom and Auntie Joanna gave me some contacts for cousins, aunts, and uncles who lived on the reservation. I reached out to all of them, but none of the contacts worked.

It was so interesting arriving at the reservation. The landscape changed from flat, boring, and monotonous to beautiful green hills, giant trees, and expansive lakes. I saw signs on the side of the road with my mother's maiden name, and figured I would just pull in and start asking around, you know, if anyone knew so-and-so. It blew my mind how much the Native people reminded me of my mom, and also the people that I had met in Hawaii. I feel that the indigenous culture is quite similar wherever you go in the world.

I wasn't having much luck finding any family until I pulled into the cultural center. It was a small building with Native artifacts just outside of the local casino. I walked in and asked the lady at the front desk if she happened to know anyone from my mom's family.

"Yes, of course," she said, "my sister's got that last name."

"Do you happen to know Rich? I'm looking to connect with him. I am family."

"My sister is married to Rich, but no way that's the same one."

We did this back and forth for a bit, and it turned out that while there are many folks with the same last name, my mom's cousin was, in fact, married to this lady's sister.

Rich was definitely surprised to meet me. He knew my mom and her family really well, even my grandpa who I had never met. He took me to his grave and then showed me all the burial places of our family members. He introduced me to my extended family on the reservation who I never even knew existed and helped me to officially enroll in the tribe and even to apply for, and ultimately receive, my certificate of Indian blood. There was a common thread in everyone I met. I could see the trauma that they carried, trauma that was still being passed down from generation to generation.

Rich and his wife introduced me to one of the elders in the tribe. She still practiced the traditional ways of the Chippewa people. She invited me to a sweat lodge with her and other family members. She taught me about our culture, about our history. She said that white people used to get paid for shooting Indians. They would get fifty shillings for every woman and child that they shot and one hundred shillings for each man.

What happened to the Native people is unimaginable. An entire culture being wiped out in such a short period of time. Native people still carry this trauma; you can see it in their faces, in how they carry themselves, in their souls. It presents itself in alcoholism, abuse, neglect, and gambling. It's all there. Despite all this, there is also a beauty that remains. The fighting spirit, respect for, and deep knowledge of the land are so ingrained in the DNA. I'm not sure how to describe it, but I feel something deep in my cells when I'm around

Native culture. Listening to chanting, singing, stories, and so on. I feel myself come alive around it. This blood is flowing through my veins.

The good and the bad.

[UBUD, INDONESIA —OCTOBER 2019]

Not long after I came back from the States, I started seeing someone. It was really early on, we were still friends, but we had shown interest in each other, and I was doing everything in my power to move on from focusing all my energy on Kendra. Bali is like a small town, so it was inevitable that we ran into each other. I was walking with Kendra and River one evening, one of the few times that it felt easy and comfortable. As we were making our way down the street, we bumped into the girl I was seeing.

Immediately, Kendra melted down crying. She kept harping about how this girl was stunning. She asked over and over again if we were dating or if I had slept with her. I told her the truth, we were just starting to hang out and that we had only kissed. I didn't want to be with anyone, I wanted to be with my family, but Kendra kept pushing me away. She told me it was over and that she was seeing other people, so I was trying my best to get on with my life.

Kendra was hysterical. She told me she wanted to get back together, that she wanted to be a family again. She told me if I ended things with this girl, we could make it work.

I liked the girl I was seeing, but my heart was with Kendra and River, and so I ended things with her.

I was so excited at the idea of being together again. I showed up to see River and Kendra one evening. Kendra was already standing outside, River in her arms, when I pulled up on my motorbike.

My heart was in pieces. I missed Kendra of course, but I missed River more than I could ever put in words. All I wanted was to be able to put the pieces of my family back together again, and it felt like it was finally happening.

"Hey, girls."

"Hi, Mikey."

"Hi, River," I said, walking over to my little girl. Just as I went to pick her up out of her mom's arms, she started to cry. It broke me. "It's okay. She doesn't have to if she doesn't want to," I said.

"I'm sorry, Mikey. She's tired. We've had a long day."

"I understand," I said, defeated., "So how are you feeling?"

"About what?" Kendra asked coyly, as though she hadn't had the slightest clue what I was talking about. As if we hadn't been talking about getting back together.

"About us. About working things out and sticking together as a family."

"I don't know. I don't think we can."

"Kendra, come on. We can get through this—as a family."

"I need time and space. You need to work on you."

"I am working on me. Do you understand where this is leading?"

"Everything's gonna be okay. You're gonna be okay. You'll always be River's dad," she said, dismissing me.

I snapped. I couldn't believe she was doing this. In this moment, I realized that she didn't want to be with me, but she didn't want to see me happy with someone else either. I saw myself losing everything. "Listen, you selfish fucking idiot, I'm going to lose River entirely. I'm going to lose you. I'm going to lose my family! You are throwing it all away!"

"Woah! Okay, that's it, get off the property! Get the fuck out of here now! Or I will call some men I know over to remove you!"

"What men?! You are throwing everything away! Don't you care that I will lose River?! You're so fucking selfish!!!"

"You should have thought about that! You've already lost us!"

I don't think either of us are proud of ourselves for how we handled that moment. I know I'm not. I think about that day constantly. I remember leaving on my motorbike and aimlessly driving around Bali all night. It was a wild storm, thunder and lightning covering the sounds of my agonizing screams. The rain and helmet concealing the tears streaming down my face.

~ ~ ~

A couple of days later I came back to see River, to try one last time to fix things. I pulled up and saw another guy on the property.

Feeling like a guest among my own family, I greeted him. "Hey, what's up? How's it going?"

"Hey, good, nice to meet you. I'm Miles."

"Hi. Mike," I said, shaking his hand.

"You from the States?"

"Yeah, San Diego."

"Oh really? I know a crew from Encinitas. I've spent a couple of months there."

"No way, that's right near my hometown."

"Do you know Jake and Randall?"

"Yeah! They're younger than me but I know them. Love those guys."

Just then, Kendra emerged from the house, walking over.

"Well, nice to meet you, man," Miles says, looking at Kendra and picking up on her cue to cut the conversation short.

"You too."

Kendra and I began to walk together. Once we were far enough away to talk in private, she stopped. She turned to me.

"What is this?" I asked, motioning back toward the house. Toward Miles.

"Oh," she said, almost shocked that I noticed. "He's just a friend."

I had the all-too-familiar knot in my stomach, and I knew right away that she was lying. I couldn't handle this conversation, not while he was there.

[PADANG BRIDGE, INDONESIA —OCTOBER 2019]

I was up early, another sleepless night. By now, I couldn't even remember the last time I had slept through the night. I was on the bridge looking out at the waves as Kendra pulled up. I knew that look she had. She looked like she had been up having sex all night. I knew it because at one point I was the cause of it. She was smiling, half checking the waves, half focused on her phone as she texted. She had that smile you have when you are texting a new crush.

The moment I saw it, I knew. I knew in my heart it was over; she had moved on. She kept me on the line until she had something else locked in.

Kendra spotted me. Somewhat on autopilot, she walked over to me and gave me a hug.

"Hi, Mikey. Good morning," she said, almost bashfully.

I wanted to throw up. "Good morning."

"I'm headed to work. Just wanted to say hello. Enjoy your day." She paused. "Oh, and I should tell you, so you don't hear it from somebody else. I'm seeing Miles now. I didn't think there was anything between us, but there is. We're spending time together now. I have to go. I'll speak to you soon. I just wanted you to know."

Kendra proceeded to tell me that her decision really had nothing to do with everything that came up with River. She told me that, for her, it was over back when she checked my search history. She said the moment she saw that I talked to my friends about our relationship and that I was looking up my exes, she lost all hope for me. She went on to say our separation had nothing to do with me not loving her, nothing to do with River, or the project we were building. I realized she created all of these issues just to pick fights because she didn't love me anymore.

I was in shock. There was nothing to say. I had already known it was over when I saw Miles at the house, I had known it when I saw her pull up that morning, but now it had been said out loud. Top that off with her telling me that it had nothing to do with our daughter and it felt like I was falling down a deep hole at uncontrollable speeds. I honestly thought that I had experienced all the levels of pain that existed in the world, but I was wrong. I felt the world spinning out of control. I felt the most excruciating emotional pain imaginable—the reality of losing my family brought back all the fear and pain of my own childhood. The pain of losing my parents. This was too much for me to handle.

I got on my motorbike and drove.

I ended up at a friend's house and crashed in his guest room.

I have no idea how long I was there. I curled up in the fetal position and cried until I had nothing left in my body. I began pacing around the room, unsure of what to focus on, what to do. The pain became so unbearable that I didn't know what else to do but to meditate, the closest way to escape reality without taking drugs.

I put on my headphones and listened to guided meditations for one hour at a time. I let the calming music and voice of the guide drown out the world. I kept coming back to this space, to this meditation, over and over. Into the third hour, and during this time of the greatest emotional pain and suffering I have ever experienced, I broke through some mental barrier.

There was a moment when I was experiencing complete peace and bliss like I had taken some divine version of ecstasy.

I felt it in my heart.

The experience really doesn't translate into words. It wasn't like other things that came from my imagination; this came from someplace else. It was otherworldly. In my mind's eye, I saw a white horse with wings, with the sun behind it. Tears streamed down my face as I received a message that most suffering is a choice. In that moment, I realized that everything I had been through, the good and the bad, was all an initiation to get to a point of learning how to self-regulate my emotions. I felt connected to myself and to life like never before. Although I didn't take any drugs, I was high for the rest of the day. I kept wondering, *How does that even happen?* When I read this, it is embarrassing and comes off as cringey, but this experience was incredibly profound for me.

[CANGGU, INDONESIA —DECEMBER 2019]

Through healing, I began to rebuild my life again in a healthy way.

Kendra and I were figuring out how to navigate co-parenting, and River would spend the weekends with me.

Every weekend I would do my best to soak up our time together, to spoil her, and to make sure we had as much fun together as possible. Our favorite activity was going to Waterbom Bali, the local waterpark. I would put her in her wetsuit—I couldn't believe how tiny it was—and then slip her arms into the floaties. There were water cannons, slides, wheels, ropes, and giant dump buckets. We would play there for hours. It felt as though we could both stay in the water forever—like it was the happiest place in the world for her as well.

It was still hard for me. I was grateful that Kendra was letting River spend the weekends with me, but I was still navigating how to be a single dad while still dealing with the pain of losing the traditional family unit. I was learning how to accept Kendra's decision and figuring out a new way to build a relationship with my daughter.

This period of time was crucial for my personal development and growth. I was learning how to self-regulate my emotions, which I didn't even know was possible. I had learned and accepted that I was not a victim of my life and that out of chaos comes opportunity. I became really inspired as I came more into acceptance of what happened, and I was looking forward to the future, what I wanted to create, and the type of dad I was becoming.

[PRESENT DAY]

When the pandemic hit in early 2020, Kendra called me to tell me that she had decided to leave Bali with her new partner and ride out the pandemic from Australia. There was no discussing it, she had already made the decision, and I had no say in the matter. Since we weren't married, I wasn't able to get into Australia as an American. I can't tell you the rage that I felt toward her. I knew in my heart that I wasn't going to see my daughter for a long time. I might not have been a perfect father, but I wanted to be part of River's life, to raise her and watch her grow up, even if that meant sharing the responsibility with Kendra. I didn't think I could go through more loss and devastation, but here I was. After going through yet another breakdown, and getting myself stable again, I decided to fly back to the States. This was after living in Indonesia for roughly ten years. It was scary as hell.

March 26, 2020, at the ultimate peak of fear on our planet. The airport in Bali was almost completely locked down. I got on one of the last few flights out of the country. When I landed in LA, the city was a ghost town. I never planned on being back there and wasn't sure what I was going to do. It might sound selfish, but at a certain point, I started enjoying the pandemic. I said, *Fuck it*, and I decided to let go of any fear of getting COVID-19. At that point it felt like my life had already been fucked for over twenty years, so there was no real difference between "normalcy" and pandemic life. I actually felt like I was thriving, and my attitude toward people who were living in terror was, *Welcome to the party!*

In coming home, I had to swallow big chunks of truth about myself. After finally getting health insurance, for the first time in over twenty years, I learned that I had suffered brain damage from all the drug and alcohol use in addition to the multiple concussions from surfing over the years. I was also diagnosed with ADHD and depression at the age of thirty-eight. After struggling for so long in many different areas of my life and ending up at yet another bottom, in a way, I became open to taking medication. I never in my life thought that I would take antidepressants. But after hitting another bottom in sobriety, I learned that the body shuts down and goes into a depression on purpose, as a way to protect itself and force a reset, when it's been in fight-or-flight for so long. I took the meds for a year, and they helped get me out of a rut. When I felt like it was time, I got off of them. I don't ever want to be in a position where I rely on something like that to function. Let's just say something happens, and I'm not able to get the meds, then what? I'm fucked. All that to say, the meds served a purpose in pulling me out of the headspace I was in and helped get me to where I am today. It hasn't been easy. I'm up and down every day. It's a constant battle of light and dark in my mind. A battle between the immature, little child and the grown man. I am definitely more compassionate toward people who choose to take these meds, whether it be veterans or people like my parents who have suffered from lifelong traumas.

In swallowing my pride, I also found a job working in a rehab as a sober companion. It wasn't something I planned to do, but my options were to take that job or be homeless. Sink or swim, and I have always found a way to stay afloat. By now, I had been out of the drug and alcohol world and sober for so long that I didn't even know what fentanyl was. I soon found out. One of the clients was a disaster. As I showed up on shift, one of the staff members was concerned there was some suspicious behavior going on with some of the clients. This one client in particular locked himself in one of the bathrooms. The staff members knocked on the door over and over without any response. After a short time, we kicked down the bathroom door to find the client on the floor. I can't describe to you what it's like to witness someone firsthand who is OD'ing on fentanyl. His head was massive, inflamed, and completely purple. We immediately started CPR, trying to resuscitate him. We Narcaned him—no response. The paramedics and firefighters arrived and did everything they could. He died right there.

In the chaos of everything going on, one of the firefighters accidentally pricked himself with a needle on the floor. He was panicked, as anyone would be. He was asking all of us whether or not the client had any preexisting health issues. We couldn't really do anything to calm his nerves, but it opened my eyes to what first responders go through on a daily basis when they are doing everything they can to save lives. All I can say is that I hope he was okay.

The aftermath of the client's passing was a heart-wrenching process. The man's father flew in from Florida to talk to us about his son's last moments. This young man had been to over thirty treatment centers by the age of thirty-six. It had been a long, hard battle. He left behind a three-year-old son. It's just senseless, this father having to bury his child, a kid never having the chance to get to know his own dad. What's going on in this country with fentanyl and other drugs on the market, new and old alike, is insane to me. My hope is that someone picks up this book in a rehab or in a school somewhere, and they see what is possible if we stay sober and find something we love doing. It doesn't mean it's gonna be easy, obviously, but you'll have a shot.

Looking back on my surfing days, when I lost all my sponsors, I couldn't imagine I had any chance at a life worth living. That changed when I got sober. I still wanted to see the world. I wasn't going to let anyone or anything stop me. I decided that I was going to do it on my own steam, with zero backing from anyone or anything. I would work in each country as I went. Through resilience and sheer determination, I was able to live my dream traveling the world, surfing the most exotic waves, meeting incredible people, learning about different cultures, and most importantly, having my daughter and learning about myself. Without my sobriety, none of this would have been possible.

Circling the globe and living abroad didn't solve everything for me. I still faced challenges along the way, some of which nearly killed me. In all of these years of struggle, I feel like I tried everything to mend my mind. From breathwork and meditation to following gurus, going between being vegan and being a carnivore, seeing energy workers, even becoming agnostic for a period of time—I was willing to do whatever it took to get better, to heal. In their own way, all of these things were helpful for a short period of time, but in the end, I would always get completely slammed by life, again. It's really only been AA and the fellowship that has consistently been there for me in all respects.

Throughout all of this, my parents were always on my mind. Growing up and as a young man, it was hard to watch my parents experience a life of suffering. The constant upheaval and, oftentimes, misery was unbearable to witness. It felt as though they were in anguish every day. It ate at me when they were living in their car, struggling to get by. When I came back to LA, I was relieved to see that things had shifted for them. They were able to get into government-subsidized housing, which sounds worse than it is. They were the first ones to move into a brand-new one-bedroom apartment, near the coast. Having a home has been a game changer for them, as it would be for anyone. They have a place to call their own, a place to shower and rest. It's a simple life. They cook meals at home and have a new child, Henry, a long-haired wiener dog. They spend every moment doting on him. That dog has changed their lives and has brought so much love and joy to my parents. It's incredible how animals can do that. The thing that blows me away the most is that my dad is creeping up on one year sober, and my parents seem to be okay. I talk to them weekly and tell them that I love them every chance I get.

[EPILOGUE]

At night, I dream about my daughter. I have seen countless scenarios play out in my mind about how we will meet again and when it will happen. There is one dream that I often come back to. I see her and I immediately see so much of myself in her, her love of the ocean, her sense of adventure; it's all there.

So there we are, in Uluwatu. River sits in a café overlooking the surf. She has come to Bali after reading my journal, booking a flight on a whim with no plan at all. I am here hosting a recovery-based surf retreat, a give-back program for those who cannot afford treatments or rehabs. River takes in her surroundings, sipping her tea as she scrolls through photos of me, making sure she knows exactly what I look like, similar to the way I held my dad's photo when I was nine years old.

She sees a group setting up on the sand. She can tell by how they carry their boards that they are new to surfing. Through the group of people, she spots me. She watches me from afar, observing how I move, the way I interact with the clients, seeing herself in the shape of my smile.

I kneel down in the sand, untangling the leashes, wondering how the clients even got them in these knots in the first place. I am focused on the task at hand, yet somehow I feel her presence. I think to myself that of course I feel her presence here in Bali—this is where she was born. I feel a wave of peace come over my heart.

A shadow forms in the sand in front of me. As I look up, I see the eyes of my daughter locked with my own.

THE END

AFTERWORD

I really didn't want to write this book. Trust me, I had no intentions of it. Sometimes I think I shouldn't be doing all of this or what difference can I really make. That's the weak voice; that's the loser. If you approach something as an act of service, how can you go wrong? That's my intent, to reach the man that I used to be, the man that I still am some days.

Sometimes I wonder how I've walked through so much turmoil in sobriety. I have walked through all of the things that my dad walked through, only I did it sober. Without this, things would have been another level of horrific, just like they were for my mother and father. Epigenetic science talks about how it's the environment that affects the gene. Trauma had become part of my cells without me even knowing how it happened. I can't describe to you how sorry I am for what came up in me. I think about it constantly, why it happened, and how I could possibly fix it. It ate at me enough so that I began to dream up ways to end my own life. Instead, I chose a living amends to my daughter.

Being sober doesn't mean you're not going to walk through pain and that life is going to be rosy. It just means that you'll be able to walk through those things with a sober mind, which could mean life or death for many. It does for me. When I tell my partner about the things that I've walked through in life, she constantly says that she can't believe I'm still alive. I have walked through more pain in sobriety than I did when I was drinking and using, and now that I'm on the other side of it, there's something beautiful about experiencing the wide range of human emotions without numbing it with drugs or alcohol. I despised walking through that pain while I was in it, but now that I'm on the other side of those periods of my life, I do see beauty in it.

Seeing beauty or lessons in the pain doesn't mean that things have come easy for me. I can't tell you how much I have felt like a failure in my life. At certain points, it has felt like I'm not allowed to experience success. Time and time again it seems good things have happened in my life, or I would build something up, only for it to collapse, or for me to burn it to the ground in self-sabotage. All the while, I have seen peer after peer experience massive success. It's like God has sent me to the end of the line. I haven't given up. Who knows, maybe me thinking God has sent me to the end of the line is actually him putting me in the front of the line without me knowing it, all through the vessel of this book. Time will tell. I'm just thankful to have moments of peace today.

Bill Wilson, the founder of AA, wrote a letter in 1958 called *Emotional Sobriety: The Next Frontier* when he was over twenty years sober. I relate to it so much and it is refreshing for me to hear that the founder of AA faced similar struggles with long-term sobriety. Look it up if any of this resonates.

Emotional sobriety is just one aspect of my life that has

helped me to become the person I am today, and in turn, has helped me bring this story to life. I have shifted my beliefs and my way of thinking. I believe that we are in a spiritual war on this planet. I have experienced things so dark that you cannot convince me otherwise. I'm not here to pretend like I'm some religious person, but I had some things happen in my life that led me to get baptized in Christ on August 27, 2023. I have always believed in God or a higher power but never expected to find myself going to church or being baptized.

This change was brought on by two pretty incredible older men who had come into my life. It's somewhat simple, really; they openly believe in Christ, and they have what I want. When I say they have what I want, I mean that they are humble, family men, good fathers, and good husbands. They are peaceful, safe human beings who are there for others. It's not only that though. They have a light pouring out of them that is hard to put into words. There is a light of peace and humility that emanates from them. What's really interesting is that these two men didn't know each other; they were from different countries but they came into my life at the same time. They had beautiful lives and an energy around them that echoed that. They had wives and children who loved them, they were creative, financially stable, and owned their homes. They weren't ultra-wealthy men, but they were comfortable.

The first man I met was a professional athlete and a womanizer in his younger days. He mentioned how empty, painful, and lonely that path was. It wasn't until he committed his life to Christ and said he was going to do the right thing that things finally shifted for him. After that, he met a woman he really liked and dated her for a year. He said he didn't kiss this woman until their wedding day. This caught me off guard. In the past, I had been with women in less than five minutes of meeting them. At the same time, I met another beautiful soul. This man was almost forty when he decided to make a change and he, too, didn't kiss his wife until their wedding day. Synchronicity at its finest. I heard these two stories at a time when I was absolutely defeated by relationships. Feeling like I gave my heart and soul to partners only for them to abandon the relationship. I played my part, don't get me wrong. There is zero power in victimhood.

To the best of my ability, I have been walking with Christ for the past year, and slowly but surely my life is getting better. No, I didn't meet a woman and date her for a year before kissing her at our wedding. But, I have a girlfriend, Dani, now who loves me for who I am, and I love her. This is pretty incredible after thinking that I would never have the capacity to love again after the things I have experienced in relationships. I have never been able to be myself like I am around her. She is a force for good and has my back. I could go to war with this woman. This book would not have seen the light of day without her. This is the first time in my life that I've had the space and support to not be in survival but step into my creativity and write this book. Trust me, I had a lot of help, and that's putting it lightly. There is something about being accepted for who you are entirely, for being in a safe environment both in a relationship and a home, that gives space for creativity.

Even with all that, I still have a hard time with the day-to-day at times. I feel numb a lot when things are good. It's not just when food and shelter are taken care of, it's stability in general. It seems I am best when shit hits the fan because I kick it into gear and get into action. I jokingly say to Dani, "Everything would be fine if a tsunami was hitting right now," because I know I would be on the move, trying to help people get to safety. That's just how I'm wired. I thrive in calamity. It's when everything is good or boring that I struggle. I've had to learn to find ways to be okay with life being good because, come to find out, I'm usually not.

I jokingly say, "I've tried everything else, so why not try Christ?" More than ever, I truly feel like I don't know anything. Dani hates it when I say that, but it seems that as soon as I start getting cocky and confident in the way I think the world works, I get slammed again. So I truly feel like I don't know anything, and maybe that's the way God wants it—all the things I say are my learnings, and I hope to bring more awareness around these subjects. Dani prefers it when I say, "More shall be revealed," and isn't that true? We don't know what's coming, but more is coming, that we can be sure of. Don't ever give up, because you never know when life is teeing you up to put you in a better position than you were in before, even though it may be terrifying in this moment.

I feel like I'm in a place where I realize that God had to take me down every type of path to show me what doesn't work, to show me that there is only one true path.

"God never uses someone greatly until he tests them deeply."

—ATTRIBUTED TO A.W. TOZER

I, like you, am still being tested.
—Michael S. Millin

ACKNOWLEDGMENTS

Alcoholics Anonymous, there have been many periods when I had no one to turn to. It was Alcoholics Anonymous that became my family from a young age. AA has raised me, in a way, and is still raising me to this day. It's taught me how to strive to have integrity, morals, and how to make things right when I mess up. It's taught me that I have to find ways to be of service to humanity if I wanna experience any sort of fulfillment in this life. Members of AA have given freely to me, asking nothing in return. All they ask is that I pass it on to the next person. It's crazy to think of what I thought AA was, compared to what it actually is. I will be giving back to AA and recovery for as long as I am alive. It's by far been the most stable and powerful thing I've been a part of.

Danielle Makenna Forras, what can I say? You brought me and this dream from the grave into physical form. I have never met someone with the strength of character that you possess. The perfect balance of Dreamer and Doer. You are beautiful and smart, and I am so thankful that you came into my life. I know I tell you this all the time, but I truly feel that God sent you to me. I love you.

My mom and dad, Michael and Sandra Millin. I know you guys did your best. My childhood was a nightmare at times, just like your childhoods were. It took me a long time to realize it was all a blessing, in some sick, fucked-up way. I know at your core that you always loved me, and that is more than a lot of sons and daughters ever get. I will always love you for that. Thank you for having the strength to power through. It makes me so happy to know that you are experiencing some peace in your later years.

Tom Kelly and his wife, Lauren, thank you for being one of the best mentors to have ever come into my life. I will never forget what you did for me. You showed me how a normal family operates and what it's like to live a life with high moral standards. You asked for nothing in return.

The Baugh family, you were a strong inspiration for me in early sobriety, showing me how to live a clean, healthy life. Thomas Baugh, thank you for bringing food to my parents when they were living in their car; you were teaching me what it's like to show people unconditional love by doing that. It meant a lot to me. Critter and Sara, thank you for being great influences on me in a time when I really needed it.

Nicholas Jon Schwaebe, you are like a father to me, in your own way. I will always be grateful for everything that you've done for me. Your discipline and ability to keep surfing is inspiring and something that is rarely seen in someone in their late seventies. A true freak of nature. Thank you for all of your support.

Aunt Donna, you were always my favorite auntie. Thank you for being someone who was always kind and safe to be around.

Adam Instone, you are one of the most unique dudes I've ever met. Thank you for being you, and for being an important stepping stone to a better way of life.

Drew Thurm, you've been a friend that I can count on. You've been there for the lowest of lows in the most compassionate way. Your generosity and sense of humor are one of a kind. Thank you, brother. Drink some cement and harden up!

Jordan Will Partie, thank you for your incredible sense of humor and for showing me how to keep the best parts of me alive in sobriety.

Although I have never met Theo Von or David Goggins, I owe you both a thank-you.

Theo Von, I truly believe you are a healer. You've had the ability to make me laugh when going through the deepest of pain.

David Goggins, I've always turned to your work when at a rock bottom. You have a way of pushing someone to put it in 4X4 to get out of a rut.

Jamie Cappelletti, Holly Gorman, Jeff Guillot, Maggie Rains, and Mark Chait of Scribe Media. Thank you for helping us bring this book to life. You guys had a no-bullshit attitude from the start that we appreciate more than you can imagine. It was a pleasure working with you.